Alia Bano

Shades

Methuen Drama

Published by Methuen Drama 2009

1 3 5 7 9 10 8 6 4 2

Methuen Drama
A & C Black Publishers Limited
36 Soho Square
London W1D 3QY
www.methuendrama.com

ISBN 978 1 408 11523 7

A CIP catalogue record for this book is available from
the British Library

Typeset by Country Setting, Kingsdown, Kent
Printed and bound in Great Britain by
CPI Cox and Wyman, Reading, Berkshire

ROYAL COURT

The Royal Court Theatre presents

SHADES

by **Alia Bano**

First performance at the Royal Court Jerwood Theatre Upstairs,
Sloane Square, London, on 28 January 2009.

Supported by

The Young Writers Festival is supported by
John Lyon's Charity
with additional funding from
The John Thaw Foundation *and*
The D'Oyly Carte Charitable Trust

27 February – 21 March

young writers festival
a miracle
by Molly Davies

ROYAL COURT

Take one baby and a mother who's not sure if she's ready. Add a soldier returned from war and a grandmother holding the fort. Mix in a landscape of flatness and a pinch of violence in the countryside and maybe, just maybe, you'll get a miracle.

Supported by

JOHN LYON'S CHARITY

020 7565 5000 Tickets £15 (£10 concs)
www.royalcourttheatre.com

With additional funding from
the John Thaw Foundation

SHADES
by **Alia Bano**

Cast in order of appearance

Sabrina **Stephanie Street**
Zain **Navin Chowdhry**
Ali **Elyes Gabel**
Mark **Matthew Needham**
Reza **Amit Shah**
Nazia **Chetna Pandya**

Director **Nina Raine**
Designer **Lucy Osborne**
Lighting Designer **Matt Drury**
Sound Designer **David McSeveney**
Casting Director **Amy Ball**
Assistant Director **Nessah Muthy**
Production Manager **Tariq Rifaat**
Stage Managers **Carla Archer, Lucy Taylor**
Costume Supervisor **Jackie Orton**

THE COMPANY

ALIA BANO (Writer)

Alia Bano studied English at Queen Mary, University of London, and taught A Level and GCSE English in Haringey. She joined the Royal Court's Young Writers' Programme in 2004. Her early work was read at Theatre Royal, Stratford East during the BritAsia Festival in 2005. She was subsequently invited to join Soho Theatre's Core Writing Group, and took part in the Royal Court's Unheard Voices programme in 2008. Her verbatim play Behind the Image, developed with Nina Raine, was presented during the Royal Court Rough Cuts season in 2008.

NAVIN CHOWDHRY (Zain)

FOR THE ROYAL COURT: Behind the Image Rough Cut.

OTHER THEATRE INCLUDES: Much Ado About Nothing (Globe); Mashed (Bristol Old Vic); Hijra (London New Play Festival).

TELEVISION INCLUDES: Free Agents, NY-LON, Sinchronicity, Golden Hour, New Tricks, Dr Who, Teachers (regular), Waking the Dead, Judge John Deed, City Central, Bangra Heads, Skin Deep, The Insiders, Dalziel and Pascoe, Ruth Rendell Mysteries – The Double, Gulliver's Travels, Casualty, Crown Prosecutor, London's Burning.

FILM INCLUDES: Skellig, Red Mercury, The Seventh Coin, Le Collier Perdu de la Colombe, King of the Wind, Madame Sousatzka, A Chaat in the Park, Seafood, On a Life's Edge, Landmark, Surviving Sabu.

RADIO INCLUDES: Stretch.

MATT DRURY (Lighting)

FOR THE ROYAL COURT: Birth of a Nation, The Mother.

OTHER THEATRE INCLUDES: Private Lives, Same Time Next Year, Absent Friends, Absurd Person Singular, Deadly Nightcap, Bedroom Farce, Sweet Revenge, Joking Apart, Dead Certain, Cinderella, Dangerous Obsession, Spider's Web (Theatre Royal Windsor); Under Their Hats, (Thorndike Theatre, Leatherhead & West End), Nicholas Nickleby, The Hollow Crown, Guys and Dolls, (Thorndike Theatre, Leatherhead); The Flipside, Shirley Valentine, The Gentle Hook (Bill Kenwright); Fools Rush In (UK Tour); Funny Money (UK Tour); Two of A Kind (UK Tour); Catch Me if You Can (UK Tour); Framed (National); Cassie (Everyman, Cheltenham); Scooping the Pot (UK Tour); Daemons (European Tour); The Hollow (UK Tour), The Unexpected Guest (UK Tour); The Haunted Hotel (UK Tour); Arsenic and Old Lace (UK Tour); An Ideal Husband (UK Tour).

Matt is Head of Lighting at the Royal Court.

ELYES GABEL (Ali)

FOR THE ROYAL COURT: Borderline.

OTHER THEATRE INCLUDES: Prince of Delhi Palace (National); Headstones (Arcola); Mr Elliott (Chelsea Theatre); Fragile Land (Hampstead).

TELEVISION INCLUDES: Waterloo Rd, Dead Set, Apparitions, Casualty, Doctors, I Love Mummy.

FILM INCLUDES: Boogeyman, Kingdom of Dust.

RADIO INCLUDES: The Secret of Iguando, The Projectionist.

DAVID McSEVENEY (Sound Designer)

FOR THE ROYAL COURT: The Girlfriend Experience (& Theatre Royal Plymouth), Contractions, Fear & Misery/War & Peace.

OTHER THEATRE INCLUDES: Gaslight (Old Vic); Charley's Aunt, An Hour and a Half Late (Theatre Royal Bath); A Passage to India, After Mrs Rochester, Madame Bovary (Shared Experience); Men Should Weep, Rookery Nook (Oxford Stage Company); Othello (Southwark Playhouse).

OTHER THEATRE AS ASSISTANT DESIGNER: The Permanent Way (Out of Joint); My Brilliant Divorce, Auntie and Me (West End); Accidental Death of an Anarchist (Donmar).

ORIGINAL MUSIC: The BFG (Secret Theatre Productions).

David is Sound Deputy at the Royal Court.

MATTHEW NEEDHAM (Mark)

Matthew is making his professional stage debut in Shades.

TELEVISION INCLUDES: Casualty (Regular)

LUCY OSBORNE (Designer)

THEATRE INCLUDES Macbeth (Edinburgh Lyceum/Nottingham Playhouse); The Broken Space Festival, 2,000 Feet Away, Tinderbox and The dYsFUnCKshOnalZ (Bush); Artefacts (Nabakov Theatre Company/ Bush/Brits off Broadway, New York); Some Kind of Bliss (Trafalgar Studios/Brits off Broadway Festival, New York); Be My Baby (New Vic Theatre); Rope (Watermill); Closer (Theatre Royal Northampton); The Long and the Short and The Tall (Sheffield Lyceum); The Prayer Room (Birmingham Rep/Edinburgh Festival Fringe); Ship of Fools (Theatre 503); The Tempest (Box Clever National Tour); The Unthinkable (Sheffield Crucible Studio); Almost Blue (Riverside Studios); Dr Faustus (The Place); Mariana Pineda (BADA); Touch Wood (Stephen Joseph Theatre); Breaker Morant (Edinburgh Festival Fringe); Richard III (Cambridge Arts); Flight Without End, Lysistrata, Othello (LAMDA); Generation (Gate Theatre); Season of Migration to the North (RSC New Writing Season).

CHETNA PANDYA (Nazia)

THEATRE INCLUDES: A Disappearing Number (Complicite International Tour); Deadeye (Kali); Coram Boy (National); Lucky Stiff (New Wimbledon Studios); Romeo & Juliet (Changeling Theatre Company).

TELEVISION INCLUDES: Holby Blue, Broken News, The Worst Week of My Life, Green Wing, The Message, New Tricks, Doctors.

RADIO INCLUDES: A Disappearing Number, Bora Bistra.

NINA RAINE (Director)

FOR THE ROYAL COURT: **Behind The Image Rough Cut.**

OTHER THEATRE INCLUDES: Unprotected (Liverpool Everyman/Traverse); Rabbit (Old Red Lion Theatre/Trafalgar Studios/59East59 Theatre, New York) Vermillion Dream (Salisbury Playhouse); Eskimo Sisters (Southwark).

RADIO INCLUDES Alan Howard Reads.

AWARDS INCLUDE: 2006 Best Director TMA Award, 2006 Amnesty International Freedom of Expression Award, 2006 Evening Standard Award for Most Promising Playwright; 2006 Critics Circle Award for Most Promising Playwright.

AMIT SHAH (Reza)

FOR THE ROYAL COURT: **Free Outgoing.**

OTHER THEATRE INCLUDES: A Christmas Carol (Rose, Kingston); The Hour We Knew Nothing Of Each Other, The Man of Mode, The Alchemist, The Life of Galileo, The Royal Hunt of the Sun (National); The Hot Zone (Lyric Hammersmith); 24 Hour Plays (Old Vic); Twelfth Night (West End); Bombay Dreams (West End).

TELEVISION INCLUDES: Down The Line, The Palace (regular); Honest (regular); Lead Balloon, Afternoon Play: Are You Jim's Wife?, Life Begins III.

FILM INCLUDES: 13 Semesters, Like Minds, The Blue Tower.

RADIO INCLUDES: The Second Chance, Silver Street, Raj Quartet.

STEPHANIE STREET (Sabrina)

THEATRE INCLUDES: The Scarecrow and His Servant (Southwark Playhouse); Sweet Cider (Arcola); Not the End of the World (Bristol Old Vic); Too Close to Home (Lyric Hammersmith); The Laramie Project (Kit Productions); The Vagina Monologues (UK Tour); Dark Meaning Mouse (Finborough); Strictly Dandia (Tamasha); As You Like It (Greenwich Observatory); Arabian Nights (ATC).

TELEVISION INCLUDES: Monday Monday, Apparitions, Never Better, Eastenders, Primeval, Commander III, Soundproof, Coming Up 2005: Heavenly Father, Holby City, Nylon, Doctors, 20 Things to Do Before You're 30, Red Cap, The Last Detective.

RADIO INCLUDES: Whose Sari Now, Legacy, Westway.

JERWOOD
NEW PLAYWRIGHTS

Since 1994 Jerwood New Playwrights has contributed to over fifty new plays at the Royal Court including Joe Penhall's SOME VOICES, Mark Ravenhill's SHOPPING AND FUCKING (co-production with Out of Joint), Ayub Khan Din's EAST IS EAST (co-production with Tamasha), Martin McDonagh's THE BEAUTY QUEEN OF LEENANE (co-production with Druid Theatre Company), Conor McPherson's THE WEIR, Nick Grosso's REAL CLASSY AFFAIR, Sarah Kane's 4.48 PSYCHOSIS, Gary Mitchell's THE FORCE OF CHANGE, David Eldridge's UNDER THE BLUE SKY, David Harrower's PRESENCE, Simon Stephens' HERONS, Roy Williams' CLUBLAND, Leo Butler's REDUNDANT, Michael Wynne's THE PEOPLE ARE FRIENDLY, David Greig's OUTLYING ISLANDS, Zinnie Harris' NIGHTINGALE AND CHASE, Grae Cleugh's FUCKING GAMES, Rona Munro's IRON, Richard Bean's UNDER THE WHALEBACK, Ché Walker's FLESH WOUND, Roy Williams' FALLOUT, Mick Mahoney's FOOD CHAIN, Ayub Khan Din's NOTES ON FALLING LEAVES, Leo Butler's LUCKY DOG, Simon Stephens' COUNTRY MUSIC, Laura Wade's BREATHING CORPSES, Debbie Tucker Green's STONING MARY, David Eldridge's INCOMPLETE AND RANDOM ACTS OF KINDNESS, Gregory Burke's ON TOUR, Stella Feehily's O GO MY MAN, Simon Stephens' MOTORTOWN, Simon Farquhar's RAINBOW KISS, April de Angelis, Stella Feehily, Tanika Gupta, Chloe Moss and Laura Wade's CATCH, Mike Bartlett's MY CHILD and Polly Stenham's THAT FACE.

In 2008 Jerwood New Playwrights supported THE PRIDE by Alexi Kaye Campbell, SCARBOROUGH by Fiona Evans, OXFORD STREET by Levi David Addai and GONE TOO FAR! by Bola Agbaje.

The Jerwood Charitable Foundation is a registered charity dedicated to imaginative and responsible funding of the arts and other areas of human endeavour and excellence.

Levi David Addai's OXFORD STREET
(Photo: Tristram Kenton)

Alexi Kaye Campbell's THE PRIDE
(Photo: Stephen Cummiskey)

THE ENGLISH STAGE COMPANY
AT THE ROYAL COURT

*'For me the theatre is really a religion or way of life.
You must decide what you feel the world is about and
what you want to say about it, so that everything in
the theatre you work in is saying the same thing ...
A theatre must have a recognisable attitude. It will
have one, whether you like it or not.'*

George Devine, first artistic director of the
English Stage Company: notes for an unwritten
book.

photo: Stephen Cummiskey

As Britain's leading national company dedicated to new work, the Royal Court Theatre produces new plays of the highest quality, working with writers from all backgrounds, and addressing the problems and possibilities of our time.

"The Royal Court has been at the centre of British cultural life for the past 50 years, an engine room for new writing and constantly transforming the theatrical culture." Stephen Daldry

Since its foundation in 1956, the Royal Court has presented premieres by almost every leading contemporary British playwright, from John Osborne's *Look Back in Anger* to Caryl Churchill's *A Number* and Tom Stoppard's *Rock 'n' Roll*. Just some of the other writers to have chosen the Royal Court to premiere their work include Edward Albee, John Arden, Richard Bean, Samuel Beckett, Edward Bond, Jez Butterworth, Martin Crimp, Ariel Dorfman, Christopher Hampton, David Hare, Eugène Ionesco, Ann Jellicoe, Terry Johnson, Sarah Kane, David Mamet, Martin McDonagh, Conor McPherson, Joe Penhall, Mark Ravenhill, Simon Stephens, Wole Soyinka, Polly Stenham, David Storey, Debbie Tucker Green, Arnold Wesker and Roy Williams.

"It is risky to miss a production there." Financial Times

In addition to its full-scale productions, the Royal Court also facilitates international work at a grass roots level, developing exchanges which bring young writers to Britain and sending British writers, actors and directors to work with artists around the world. The research and play development arm of the Royal Court Theatre, The Studio, finds the most exciting and diverse range of new voices in the UK. The Studio runs playwriting groups including the Young Writers Programme, Critical Mass for black, Asian and minority ethnic writers and the bi-annual Young Writers Festival For further information, go to www.royalcourttheatre.com/ywp

"Yes, the Royal Court is on a roll. Yes, Dominic Cooke has just the genius and kick that this venue needs... It's fist-bitingly exciting." Independent

PROGRAMME SUPPORTERS

The Royal Court (English Stage Company Ltd) receives its principal funding from Arts Council England, London. It is also supported financially by a wide range of private companies, charitable and public bodies, and earns the remainder of its income from the box office and its own trading activities.

The Genesis Foundation supports the Royal Court's work with International Playwrights.

The Jerwood Charitable Foundation supports new plays by new playwrights through the Jerwood New Playwrights series.

The Artistic Director's Chair is supported by a lead grant from The Peter Jay Sharp Foundation, contributing to the activities of the Artistic Director's office. Over the past ten years the BBC has supported the Gerald Chapman Fund for directors.

ROYAL COURT DEVELOPMENT ADVOCATES
John Ayton
Anthony Burton
Sindy Caplan
Cas Donald
Allie Esiri
Celeste Fenichel
Stephen Marquardt
Emma Marsh (Vice Chair)
Mark Robinson
William Russell (Chair)

PUBLIC FUNDING
Arts Council England, London
British Council
London Challenge

CHARITABLE DONATIONS
American Friends of the Royal Court Theatre
Gerald Chapman Fund
Columbia Foundation
The Sidney & Elizabeth Corob Charitable Trust
Cowley Charitable Trust
The Edmond de Rothschild Foundation*
The Dorset Foundation
The D'Oyly Carte Charitable Trust
E*TRADE Financial
Esmée Fairbairn Foundation
The Edwin Fox Foundation
Francis Finlay*
The Garfield Weston Foundation
Genesis Foundation
Haberdashers' Company
Jerwood Charitable Foundation
John Thaw Foundation
Kudos Film and Televisoin
Lloyds TSB Foundation for England and Wales
Dorothy Loudon Foundation*
Lynn Foundation
John Lyon's Charity

The Laura Pels Foundation*
The Martin Bowley Charitable Trust
Paul Hamlyn Foundation
The Peggy Ramsay Foundation
The David and Elaine Potter Foundation
Quercus Charitable Trust
Jerome Robbins Foundation*
Rose Foundation
Royal College of Psychiatrists
The Royal Victoria Hall Foundation
The Peter Jay Sharp Foundation*
Sobell Foundation
Wates Foundation

SPONSORS
BBC
Links of London
Pemberton Greenish

BUSINESS BENEFACTORS & MEMBERS
Grey London
Hugo Boss
Lazard
Merrill Lynch
Vanity Fair

INDIVIDUAL SUPPORTERS

ICE-BREAKERS
Act IV
Anonymous
Ossi & Paul Burger
Mrs Helena Butler
Cynthia Corbett
Shantelle David
Charlotte & Nick Fraser
Mark & Rebecca Goldbart
Linda Grosse
Mr & Mrs Tim Harvey-Samuel
The David Hyman Charitable Trust
David Lanch
Colette & Peter Levy

Watcyn Lewis
David Marks
Nicola McFarland
Janet & Michael Orr
Pauline Pinder
Mr & Mrs William Poeton
The Really Useful Group
Lois Sieff OBE
Gail Steele
Nick & Louise Steidl

GROUND-BREAKERS
Anonymous
Moira Andreae
Jane Attias*
Elizabeth & Adam Bandeen
Philip Blackwell
Mrs D H Brett
Sindy & Jonathan Caplan
Mr & Mrs Gavin Casey
Carole & Neville Conrad
Clyde Cooper
Andrew & Amanda Cryer
Robyn M Durie
Hugo Eddis
Mrs Margaret Exley CBE
Robert & Sarah Fairbairn
Celeste & Peter Fenichel
Andrew & Jane Fenwick
Ginny Finegold
Wendy Fisher
Hugh & Henri Fitzwilliam-Lay
Joachim Fleury
Lydia & Manfred Gorvy
Richard & Marcia Grand*
Reade and Elizabeth Griffith
Nick & Catherine Hanbury-Williams
Sam & Caroline Haubold
Mr & Mrs J Hewett
Nicholas Josefowitz
David P Kaskel & Christopher A Teano
Peter & Maria Kellner*
Mrs Joan Kingsley & Mr Philip Kingsley
Mr & Mrs Pawel Kisielewski
Varian Ayers & Gary Knisely
Rosemary Leith
Kathryn Ludlow
Emma Marsh

Barbara Minto
Gavin & Ann Neath
William Plapinger & Cassie Murray
Mark Robinson
Paul & Jill Ruddock
William & Hilary Russell
Jenny Sheridan
Anthony Simpson & Susan Boster
Brian Smith
Carl & Martha Tack
Katherine & Michael Yates

BOUNDARY-BREAKERS
John and Annoushka Ayton
Katie Bradford
Tim Fosberry
Edna & Peter Goldstein
Sue & Don Guiney
Rosanna Laurence

MOVER-SHAKERS
Anonymous
Dianne & Michael Bienes*
Lois Cox
Cas & Philip Donald
John Garfield
Duncan Matthews QC
Jan & Michael Topham

HISTORY-MAKERS
Jack & Linda Keenan*
Miles Morland
Ian & Carol Sellars

MAJOR DONORS
Daniel & Joanna Friel
Deborah & Stephen Marquardt
Lady Sainsbury of Turville
NoraLee & Jon Sedmak*

*Supporters of the American Friends of the Royal Court

FOR THE ROYAL COURT

Shades

Characters

Sabrina Khan, *Pathan*
Zain Miah, *Bengali*
Ali Mahmood, *Pakistani*
Mark Blaine, *white*
Reza Qureishi, *Pakistani*
Nazia Qureishi, *Pakistani*
Waitress (*can be doubled by the actress playing Nazia*)

Scene One

A table. A man and a woman, in a short-sleeved, quite low-cut top, are sitting opposite each other. They are in mid-conversation.

Sab Why did we come here?

Zain I'm helping you with your Bridget Jones status.

Sab They're just merging into one, IT, accountant, consultant – it's the bloody twilight zone.

Zain You could always marry me.

She laughs.

Sab They keep looking me up and down.

Zain You are dressed like the Whore of Babylon.

Sab (*looks down at her clothing*) I'm not!

Zain This is Muslim speed dating.

Sab You said I should come as I normally dress.

Zain I may have made a mistake about the clothing – overestimated the, um, ah . . . I hope you've been hiding that inquisitive mind to compensate.

Sab Shall we go home?

Zain You'll be doing the dishes for the next month. I'm not ready to leave, this is better than I thought. The ladies are lapping me up. I haven't had so much fun in ages.

Sab Of course they are. You're liberal, you're an artist – basically white, but you're brown, perfect.

Zain I've already heard a few of them give out orgasmic murmurs.

Sab *laughs.*

Zain You know you can always marry me.

Sab Ask me again at thirty.

Zain   When you're as good as dead to the Asian male – (*beat*) I'll have you.

Sab   Let's go.

Zain   Walk out midway?

Sab   Why not?

Zain   Controversial. But I'm gonna stay.

Sab   Zee.

Zain   I'm as happy as Larry.

Sab   Come on, Zee. I'm leaving.

Zain   But the guy coming up has been giving you the eye ever since we walked in.

Sab   Really?

Zain   He's quite cute.

Sab   Is he?

Zain   Uh-huh. This could be the one.

Sab *looks at him sceptically.*

Zain   He could be!

Sab   At least he'll be eye candy.

Bell rings.

Zain   Just know you have my tick of approval. Let me know how it goes.

Kisses her on the cheek just as a man in a suit appears.

Ali   *Salaam alakum.*

Sab   *Walakum salaam.*

Ali   An eager suitor?

Sab   A friend.

Ali   I'm Ali.

Sab   Sabrina.

Ali Nice to meet you. So, what do you do?

Sab I'm an events organiser. You?

Ali I'm an accountant. An events organiser – must be exciting, your job.

Sab It can be tiring, but nice seeing the finished product.

Ali So, you're a party girl.

Sab Occupational hazard.

Ali Perhaps another occupation might more suitable.

Sab You don't approve of my job?

Ali I'm sure you're very good at it.

Sab I am.

Ali You must work late nights.

Sab Sometimes.

Ali Aren't you scared as a woman / to –

Sab I get a cab on the company just like all the guys do.

Ali Can I ask you a question?

Sab Sure.

Ali Are you seriously looking?

Sab Yeah.

Ali How do you think your partner would feel about you working late?

Sab He'd understand. I would, if he needed to.

Ali I guess he would.

Quite a long pause. **Sab** *feels uncomfortable under* **Ali***'s intense stare.*

Sab What do you do in your spare time?

Ali Read, mainly history. Play football, go to the gym, do some voluntary work. You?

Sab The same, not football really.

Ali   Not really?

Sab   Unless England is playing.

Ali   'Come on England!' Even I head into a pub at that time of year.

Sab   The vibe's great! Shame it's not like that all year round.

Ali   I wouldn't know. Pubs are just a work or football thing for me.

Sab   Oh, right.

Pause.

Ali   How religious are you?

Sab   I never know how to answer that question. I mean, how do you measure religiousness?

Ali   Do you pray?

Sab   Sometimes.

Ali   Do you drink?

Sab *looks round as if she wants to escape.*

Sab   What is this, the Spanish Inquisition?

Ali   I'm just interested.

Silence.

Have you ever been in a relationship?

Sab   What?

Ali   Have you ever been out with someone?

Sab   I don't see how that's any of your business.

Ali   I just can't believe someone with your looks and dress hasn't –

Sab   Hasn't what?

Pause. **Ali** *tries to choose his words carefully.*

Ali   – attracted the attention of the opposite sex.

Sab   Right. (*Beat.*) What about you?

Ali   What about me?

Sab   Have you ever 'attracted the attention of the opposite sex'?

Ali   I don't think I'm going to answer that question.

Sab   Then neither am I.

Pause.

Ali   I think you'd look great in an Asian suit. Do you wear them?

Sab   That's a stupid question. Of course I do, sometimes.

Ali   I'm glad you said that. (*Pause.*) So, Sabrina what's your favourite food?

Sab   Why?

Bell rings.

Ali   I would love to take you to dinner, anywhere you like. It was really intriguing meeting you.

Beat. He stares at her and takes out his card from his jacket pocket.

I know this is against the process, but take my card. Call me.

Ali *exits.* **Sab** *is left by herself. She looks at the card in her hand.*

Sab   What the fuck.

Beat. A buzzer goes. Zain comes up.

Zain   Come on. Give me your matches, we've got to hand them in, they're going to email us by the end of the day.

Sab *breathes a sigh of relief, looks at the match list in her hand and begins to rip it up.* **Zain** *pulls it from her hand before she can do much damage.*

Zain   What are you doing? (*He looks at the match list.*) You haven't ticked anyone. Give me that pen.

He takes her pen and ticks all boxes.

Sab   Zain, it's not your email they're getting.

Zain   We need to know who got the most matches, remember. So what happened with Mr Cute?

Sab   Nothing.

Zain   Nothing?

Sab   He was a moron.

Zain   Ah, the condition of the Asian man! Thank God exceptions such as me exist. Shall we mingle?

Sab   Not here.

Zain   Come on then, Bridget, I'll grab a bottle from the newsagent's and then we can check who the real heartthrob is.

Blackout.

Scene Two

Back at the flat. **Sab** *is looking at the laptop,* **Zain** *is standing drinking with a glass of wine.*

Sab   I can't believe it!

Zain   Did I get more interest then you?

Sab (*looking at the laptop*)   Mr Cute!

Zain   He ticked you!

Sab   He was such a creep.

Zain   He wasn't bad-looking and he ticked you!

Sab   He was fucking intense.

Zain   Fucking intense can be good, really good.

Sab   He was the *haram* police.

Zain   Shame. They come in all disguises. He so didn't look the type. Are you sure you're not just – [*being paranoid*]?

Sab (*ironically*)   Great!

Zain   What?

Sab   He's emailed me.

Zain   Already!

He pushes her aside, picks up the laptop and walks around the flat, reading the following in a sensual tone.

'Dear Sabrina, it was delightful meeting you, don't forget to call me.' (*He wolf-whistles.*) There's no number.

Sab   He gave me his card.

Zain   You never said! God, he's keen. Call him.

Sab (*patronising tone*)   Yeah, right, Zee, I'm really going to call him.

Zain   A one-night stand with a misogynist could be fun.

Sab *chucks pillow at him. He ducks.*

Zain   You're such a prude. You should really let loose.

Sab   What, just sleep with anyone?

Zain   It's worked for me. Made me less grumpy.

Sab *chucks another pillow at him.* **Zain** *ducks, his attention to the laptop barely affected.*

Zain   Ooh, that cute little girl in the *shalwar kameez* ticked me. I may not be marrying you after all.

Sab   Great! Destined to solitude.

Zain   What exactly do you want, Sab?

Sab   You know what I want.

Zain   What?

Sab   Come on.

Zain   Seriously.

Sab   Just a normal guy.

Zain   There's plenty out there.

Sab   I just wish they were Muslim.

Zain   Stick to wanting diamonds.

Sab   I just want someone with a pulse and a brain. And that's hard to find round here.

Zain   So log onto shaadi.com

Sab   More like shag-me.com. I said pulse and brain. Can you imagine the guys that I'll meet there? Like the midget firefighter Fatimah met. Five foot four in his stockinged feet and obsessed with his sister-in-law – 'Oh, she's the perfect lady!' Anyway, I did try shaadi.com.

Zain   You never told me! I didn't know it got that bad!

Sab   Yeah, well, why would you tell anyone? I only did it for about five minutes. I was attracting the wrong types. I was attracting the really religious types, God knows why.

Zain   Just face it: you want to marry a white guy.

Sab   Marry a white guy when there's millions of Pakis about? My mother would just love that.

Zain   Rage, rage against the machine.

Sab *looks at him.*

Zain   OK, it's not easy, but make a stand.

Beat.

Sab   Don't you ever wish – [*you could tell your parents*]?

Zain   All the time, Sab.

Sab   I'm just tired.

Zain   You're getting old.

Sab   Look who's talking!

Zain   I'm a man – I have a longer shelf life.

Sab   Do you think I'm past my sell-by date?

Zain   Look, when you hit thirty, just stick on a scarf. Your marriage rating would go up –

Sab   Exponentially.

Zain   And you wouldn't have to bother with your GHD straighteners any more. Seriously – you haven't got much time left. The sell-by date is two or three years after uni. More if you do a Master's.

Sab   You get a longer shelf life if you do a Master's? I might do one!

Zain   You might need to – my sister's getting married.

Sab   She's only twenty-one! Mubarak.

Zain   You can be so traditional and blonde sometimes. Asian weddings are a pain, especially if you're single.

Sab   Tell me about it.

Zain   Who do you think will be in the firing line for the whole wedding? (*Beat.*) That's why you're coming.

Sab   Nice try, but I'm not coming.

Zain   It's a wedding, you love weddings.

Sab   I'm not going as your dummy girlfriend.

Zain   Who said anything about – ?

Sab   I don't want your mum thinking I'm the reason why you won't marry the plethora of girls she's paraded in front of you.

Zain   It's not like I haven't offered. I keep saying –

Sab   Marry you. I just might.

Blackout.

Scene Three

Zain *is pacing up and down outside a building in central London.*

Zain   Roll me a joint.

Mark   You'll smell.

Zain   She's bloody late.

Mark   It's not unusual.

Zain   Give me a cigarette.

Mark *lights cigarettes for himself and* **Zain**.

Mark   Why don't we go in without her?

Zain   I'm running the bloody thing tonight –

Mark   She'll be fine to meet us there.

Zain   I wanted her to check the roles I allocated. Let's go in. (*Smokes cigarette indecisively.*) We'll give her five minutes.

Both smoke their cigarettes.

This is the first bloody two-day festival we're organising. I just want it to be good.

Mark   It will be. She cares about the cause just as much as you do.

Zain   She promised she'd be on time.

Mark   There's nothing we can do about that now. Let's go in.

Zain   I'm going to put her with the scholar's son.

Mark   Don't do that.

Zain   I'm gonna make her regret it.

Mark   She's only a few minutes late.

Zain   It'll teach her a lesson.

Mark   She'll kill you.

Zain   No pain, no gain. A little bit of suffering might improve her timekeeping. Let's get this show on the road.

Zain *and* **Mark** *move off. A few seconds later* **Sab** *runs on in a pair of jeans and a jacket. She walks in on* **Zain**, *giving his speech. The crowd is mixed. She finds* **Mark** *and stands next to him.*

Zain   The event will take place eight weeks from today, so we haven't got long. I've designated everyone in pairings to

cater to our strengths. Remember, the more people that come,
the more awareness we raise about the injustices occurring in
the West Bank and the more money we raise for the orphanage.
There'll be a fashion show, a photography exhibition and a gala
dinner. Guys, every *job* is a self-portrait of the person who *does
it*, so let's autograph this event with our excellence.

Round of applause.

Sab He's not pissed off, is he?

Mark I calmed him down.

Sab (*gives him a kiss on the cheek*) I knew there was a reason why
I loved you. Do you know what I'm doing in regards to the
event?

Mark The fashion show. Sab, don't go mad, but as you were
late Zain's put you with this guy –

Reza Excuse me.

Mark Hi.

Reza I was sent here by the organiser, Zah, Zahid . . . ?

Mark Zain.

Reza I'm Reza Qureishi, and you're Sabrina Khan, right?

Sab Yeah.

Reza Great, I've been allocated to help you organise the
fashion show.

Sab The fashion show?

Reza Yes.

Sab With me?

Reza Yes.

Sab Fabulous. Have you done this kind of thing before?

Reza I've helped with events, not really a fashion show.

Mark There's a first time for everything.

Sab (*to* **Mark**) There really is.

Reza   I was a bit surprised to be assigned it, but Zain thought I'd be just what you needed.

Sab   Right, did he? If you're uncomfortable with the role, we can always ask –

Reza   I don't mind – it'll be a good challenge.

Sab   Yeah, it will.

Reza   Is this your first fashion – [*show too*]?

Sab (*shakes her head*)   I'm an events organiser. I'm feeling a little thirsty, I might just –

Mark   Let me get you that drink.

Sab   Thanks.

Reza   An events organiser. That's unusual for an Asian girl.

Sab   Not really.

Reza   It must be very creative.

Sab   It is.

Reza   I envy you. You're really lucky.

Sab (*surprised*)   Really?

Reza   To create something different every time. I miss that in my job.

Sab   What do you do? No, no, let me guess. You're in a suit, you could be a consultant.

Reza   In IT, perhaps?

Sab   A little too arrogant for IT.

Reza   I'm not arrogant.

Sab   You're not *arrogant* arrogant, so you're not a solicitor. I'd say an accountant.

Reza   Impressive.

Sab   The choice of occupations is limited.

Reza *laughs.*

Sab   So, you work for PWC?

Reza   Deloitte. (*Beat.*) You didn't settle on accountant because you thought I was boring?

Sab   Now you mention it –

They both laugh.

I'm sure all the Asian mums and dads are glad you're an accountant.

Reza   You don't approve of my job?

Sab   I'm sure you're very good at it.

Pause.

Reza   Are you Pakistani?

Sab   Yeah, why?

Reza   I wasn't sure. You're quite fair, you could be Arab.

Sab   We're from the North West Frontier.

Reza   That explains it then.

Sab   I gathered you were Pakistani.

Reza   It seems I'm an open book.

Sab   It seems you are.

Zain *walks in with* **Mark**.

Zain   Ah, Sabrina.

Sab   Ah, Zain!

Zain   Great, you found each other. Sab's a real star to work with, but you'll have to watch out for her timekeeping.

Sab   Zain!

Zain   It's true.

Reza   As long as we reach the end goal, I'm sure we can compromise on the timekeeping.

Mark   I couldn't agree more – compromise is key.

Sab   If only they thought like that in the Middle East, but I guess once you feel that you've been unjustifiably wronged, all you can think about is revenge.

Zain   If both sides didn't keep breaking their promises they wouldn't be in this mess.

Reza   It's terrible.

Zain   It is.

Sab   If the retaliation to the crimes was proportionate you could understand.

Mark   I'm sure both parties think they're justified.

Sab   I just don't know if there can be peace in those circumstances.

Reza   Forgiveness is the better option.

Sab   You're right, there are other methods like Gandhi, passive resistance, an organised campaign of non-cooperation.

Zain   Non-cooperation?

Sab   Imagine the person you regularly confide in, shop with, stops hanging about with you for a few months.

Mark   A few months.

Sab   You'd give in to their demands.

Reza   I'm not sure that strategy would work in the Middle East. On a personal level, sure, when my sister gives her husband the cold shoulder, he can't stand it for more than a few days. He has to apologise and take her to dinner in a nice restaurant as well.

Mark   Does that keep the peace?

Reza   *Alhumdillah.*

Sab   I'm not sure that'd work for me.

Beat.

Zain   I guess the best always demand more.

Reza   Don't tell my sister that. There'll be no – [*pleasing her*].

His phone beeps, and he quickly reads a text message.

I'm sorry, Sabrina, do you mind if we exchange numbers? My friend will be arriving in a bit, we're gonna go pray. It'll be the easiest way to get in contact.

Zain   What, praying?

Reza   No, phoning.

Mark   He was joking.

She gives **Reza** *her phone. He types his number in and hands it back.*

Sab   I'll call you now.

Reza*'s phone rings once only.*

Sab   Have you got it?

Reza *looks at his phone. While he is distracted* **Ali** *walks up behind him and taps him on the shoulder.*

Ali   I thought I'd come and get you, otherwise we're gonna miss . . . prayer.

Reza   I'll just be a minute. I'm just gonna save Sabrina's number. Everyone, this is Ali.

Ali *nods his head in acknowledgement and then extends his hand to* **Sab** *for a handshake.* **Sab** *reluctantly takes it.* **Reza** *is deep in his phone.*

Ali   Nice to meet you. (*To* **Sab**.) I believe we've met before.

Sab   Very briefly.

Zain   Wasn't it for three minutes, to be exact?

Reza   We better be going, but it was nice meeting you all. *Khudafiz.*

Ali   *Khudafiz.* (*He looks at* **Sab**.)

The spotlight follows **Reza** *and* **Ali** *as they leave.* **Ali** *gives* **Reza** *a quizzical look.*

Reza   Did they say you've met before?

Ali   In passing.

Reza   At least one of us will know what we're doing – she's an events organiser.

Ali   So you'll be working with her for the next few weeks.

Reza   Yeah.

Ali   That's great, really great.

Blackout.

Scene Four

Reza*'s house.* **Reza** *is sitting watching TV surrounded by a few magazines. He seems engrossed. He turns one of the magazines on its side and closely inspects it as if he can't believe what he's seeing. Footsteps arrive behind him. He quickly tries to hide the magazine. Enter* **Nazia**, *wearing a headscarf.*

Nazia   I thought you might be thirsty. What are you up to?

Reza   Nothing.

Nazia   Are you reading a magazine?

Reza   It's something for work.

Nazia   Boring.

Reza   Why is everyone saying that lately?

Nazia   Are you reading *Vogue*?

Reza   Where's Shoomie?

Nazia   She's asleep.

Reza   Shame.

Nazia   More like *alhumdillah*. The terrible twos are a nightmare. She threw a tantrum in Tesco's.

Reza   Why?

Nazia   I wouldn't buy her yet another Barbie.

Reza   Did she get her way, though?

Nazia   Yeah.

Reza   So she's already taking after you then.

Nazia   Are you sure that's not *Vogue*? Let me have a look.

Reza   It's just boring work – [*stuff*].

Nazia   Reza!

A pause. He hands over Vogue.

Reza   It's for research, Bhaj.

Nazia   Is that what they're calling it these days?

Reza   It's for this charity event.

Nazia   I thought your charity was raising money, not looking at naked women.

Reza   I'm organising a fashion show.

Nazia   You? (*She laughs.*)

Reza   Yeah.

Nazia   I thought you were going to do something sensible like design leaflets, PR.

Reza   The guy who organised it seemed to have made this meticulous plan and I didn't want to disrupt things.

Nazia   I hope you're not gonna – (*Taps the magazine.*)

Reza   Of course not! I was just trying to get ideas so I actually know something and I'm not a hindrance.

Nazia   Speaking of hindrances, I need a favour.

Reza   What?

Nazia   I was wondering if you would help wallpaper the house. Mum's offered, but –

Reza   Mum's offered – (*He starts to laugh.*)

Nazia   You saw what she did with the living room.

He laughs a little harder.

Reza Modern art – it's all the rage.

Nazia Reza.

Reza I'm really sorry, Bhaj, I can't. I've made plans to help out on this charity gig.

*They turn round as the door opens and **Ali** walks in.*

Nazia Ali, *salaam alakum*.

Ali Bhaji, *walakum salaam*.

Nazia How are you?

Ali Good, *alhumdillah*, busy with work.

Nazia So, you're not like Reza then – he has plenty of time on his hands.

Ali Really?

Nazia He's taken up reading –

Reza Bhaji!

Nazia He makes a good point, it's not really reading.

*She chucks **Ali** the copy of Vogue.*

Ali You're reading *Vogue*?

He flicks through the magazine and stares appreciatively at some of the shots.

Reza It's research for the fashion show.

Ali I wouldn't worry, Bhaji, the three most beautiful women I know are in this house.

Nazia *laughs.*

Nazia I'm surprised that silver tongue hasn't got you in trouble.

Ali I'm only commenting on the great beauty that Allah has created. A *sharif* boy like me only tells the truth. Don't worry, I'll make sure he isn't led astray.

Reza I can hear you, you know. I am in the room.

Nazia Yeah, look out for him, he is a bit trusting.

Ali Simple. Yeah.

Reza We can't all be as complex as you.

Nazia *Borhat mast hai.* I'm going to leave you to it. Do you want some tea, Ali?

Ali I'm cool, Bhaj.

Nazia *exits.*

Reza I can't believe what you get away with saying to my sister.

Ali Watch and learn.

Reza How's work?

Ali Big project, you know the score.

Reza Yeah.

Ali If all goes well, I'll be promoted. And get out of auditing at long last.

Reza Fantastic!

Ali So how's all with you?

Reza Work's fine, it's just this fashion show.

Ali We're still on for Friday evening, though?

Reza Of course.

Ali Great, all the guys are coming.

Reza Even Tariq?

Ali Yeah, even Tariq. Who's well under the thumb. Sometimes I don't know who the man is in that relationship. Poor sod – he thought he was safe marrying the village girl from back home . . . How wrong could he be? So, how's it going? (*Gesturing at the magazine.*)

Reza We're meeting this weekend to discuss themes. (*Tapping on* Vogue.) But this isn't really helping with sensible ones.

Ali   It's about the Middle East – why not the dress of the Muslim world?

Reza   Great idea.

Ali   Do you think so?

Reza   Yeah, I might mention it to her. Thanks, Ali.

Ali   Cool.

Reza *gets out his laptop.*

Ali   Rez, do you think it's too late to get involved?

Reza   With what?

Ali   The charity event.

Reza   That'd be great.

Ali   Yeah, and it'll all be in a good cause.

Blackout.

Scene Five

A coffee shop. **Reza** *and* **Sab** *at a table scattered with papers and photos.* **Reza** *is in a suit,* **Sab** *is in a knee-length skirt.* **Sab** *is making notes.*

Sab   You think that should be the theme?

Reza   Yeah, it just came to me. I thought it fitted with the cause.

Sab   Really?

Reza *(hesitant)*   Yeah, I mean –

Sab   It's bad enough the media has defined all Palestinians as Muslims – they're Christian, Druze, atheists . . .

Reza   Right. I didn't think.

Sab   I just hate the way everyone tries to simplify things.

Reza   I guess we better go back to the drawing board.

Sab   It should be lively and fun.

Reza   Yeah.

Sab   Something for everyone, inclusive not exclusive.

Reza   Sure.

Sab   Something that says 'summer'.

Reza   Right.

Sab   Beachwear.

Reza   Beachwear?

Sab   Uh-huh, you know – kaftan, summery skirts, bikinis. (*Beat.*) What do you say?

Reza   It's an idea.

Sab   A good one.

Reza   Don't you think . . . ?

Sab   What?

Reza   Some people might –

Sab   'Might'?

Reza   – think that's more bare than wear. (*Beat.*) And if my parents are coming, I wouldn't be able to lift my head for the shame. I don't really want to be associated with –

Sab   I was winding you up.

Reza   Right.

Sab   I was actually thinking we could do the ultimate in glamour and kitsch. Bring two worlds together.

Reza   Kitsch?

Sab   As in bad taste. (*Pause.*) You know, the plastic flowers mums decorate the living rooms with. Eastern kitsch meets Western ironic cool.

Reza (*laughs*)   God, yeah.

Sab   So, people can come in a whole range of styles.

Reza   It's a good idea.

Sab   We can have the standard three sections – daywear, evening wear and matrimonial. I was thinking that maybe we could get some –

Sound of text message arriving. **Reza** *gets his phone.*

Reza (*reads*)   Ali. Can't make it.

Sab   Shame.

Reza   He says to apologise and hopes he will be able to help out soon. He's working on this big project.

Sab (*relieved*)   You should really tell him not to stress himself out – we're fine without him.

Reza   I've made a start on the leaflets and posters. It'd be best for our budget if we went for black and white.

Sab   I'd rather we had colour. Different colours to attract the eye –

Reza   The more colours you have, the more expensive it gets.

Sab   How about we have a few shades? Black and white is so severe.

Reza   We're gonna have to cut the cost somewhere else.

Sab   Let's do that. Models – know anyone we could recruit?

Zain *walks in.*

Zain   Hiya guys. Taking my name in vain?

Sab   'Vain' being the operative word.

Reza   *Salaam alakum.*

Zain   *Walakum salaam.*

Sab   What are you doing here?

Zain   I thought I'd see how you were doing.

Sab   I was just asking Reza if he knew any models for the fashion show; we should get them early.

They share a look of amusement. **Reza** *notices.*

Zain   That's a good idea.

Sab   So?

Beat.

Reza   Actually, I might.

Zain   Really?

Sab   Great, who?

Reza   Some sisters from the Islamic centre would really be interested.

Sab   Sisters.

Reza   They'd love it, walking down the catwalk in the latest *jilbabs.*

Zain   *Jilbabs.*

He looks at **Sab** *as if to say, how could you let this happen.*

Reza   Yeah, I mean, surely we're going have a few in the show.

Sab   I don't think that really fits the theme.

Reza   We could have green, red, yellow – they'll get to flaunt their ankles. I thought we were going to cater for everyone.

Sab   I don't think –

Reza   It's financially viable. We'd make a killing. There'll be sisters in our audience and we can't let down all two of them, it would be – *(beginning to laugh)* a tragedy.

Sab   You're winding me up?

Reza *(laughs)*   Taste of your own medicine.

Zain   It was a joke.

Reza   The tickets I can take care of. Just tell me what you want.

A **Waitress** *approaches.*

Waitress   I'm sorry, but we're closing in fifteen minutes.

Reza/Sab   Thanks.

Reza   Maybe we should continue this tomorrow.

Sab   I'm working.

Reza   Thurs—

Sab   I won't be free until Saturday.

Reza   We need to decide the tickets, logo, colour. Shall we go somewhere else?

Sab   I think Brick Lounge is open.

Reza   I'd rather not go anywhere where's there's alcohol.

Sab   We can go back to mine. It's only fifteen mins away.

Reza   To yours?

Sab   Yeah, you and Mark are going to the cinema, right?

Zain   Yeah.

Reza   We'd be alone.

Sab   Yeah. We can get some work done.

Reza   I don't think it would be appropriate.

Sab   What?

Reza   I don't think it would be appropriate.

Sab   Are you winding me up?

Reza *shakes his head.*

Sab   OK.

Reza   Perhaps we should discuss it over lunch one day this week.

Sab   Sure.

Reza   I'll email you to know what lunchtimes are best for me.

Sab   OK.

Reza   *Khudafiz.*

Sab   Bye.

Zain   See you.

Reza *exits.*

Zain   I didn't know times were that desperate.

Sab   What?

Zain   You just propositioned a brother.

Sab   I didn't.

Zain (*mimics* **Sab**)   'Why don't you come back to my place, we'll be alone.'

Sab   To work.

Zain   'Would you like me to seduce you?' Do the words boy, girl and chaperone when not in public ring a bell?

Sab   Oh God!

Zain   Poor guy, you probably had him running out of here with a hard-on.

Sab   Zain!

Zain   You really should be more sensitive – he's probably had no sexual experience.

Sab   Zain!

Zain   What? I wasn't the one behaving like the local slapper.

Sab   I'm gonna have to see him again with him thinking –

Zain   Shut up, Sab. That's what I think the real problem is with these fundos.

Sab   What?

Zain   If they weren't so busy denying their sexual frustration, they'd lose all that aggression and forget about *shariah*.

Sab (*sarcastic*)   Let's turn Planet Earth into one giant orgy.

Zain   I'll have you know a man can go crazy from sexual deprivation. I came to make sure he hadn't declared *jihad* on you.

Sab (*laughs*)   You can be so stupid sometimes.

Blackout.

Scene Six

An array of clothes on hangers. **Sab** *takes off a few and puts them in front of her as if she is looking in a mirror trying them on. She picks up a long dress and begins to sway and then twirl around in it, humming a tune.* **Sab** *does not realise* **Reza** *has come back from praying. He coughs to let her know of his presence.* **Sab** *jumps and stops what she is doing.*

Sab   That was quick.

Reza   Five times every day, it gets like that.

Sab *goes back to looking through the clothes.*

Reza   What were you doing?

Sab   Looking through the clothes.

Reza   Were you dancing?

Sab   I was trying to imagine how the clothes would look down the catwalk. Nothing wrong with that.

Reza   No, there isn't.

Sab   I guess we better get on with picking what we actually want. Everything on that rail is a 'no', on this a 'yes'.

They work in silence. **Reza** *flicks through a few things and picks out a male T-shirt.*

Reza (*badly pronounced*)   *L'état, c'est moi!*

Sab   'I am the state.'

Reza   What?

Sab   '*L'état c'est moi*' – it means, 'I am the state.'

Reza   You're really knowledgeable.

Sab   I did French for A level.

Reza   I was always really terrible at French.

Sab (*looking at the top*)   Definitely a 'yes'. And that – is definitely a 'no'.

She goes to put the top on the 'yes' rail. Meanwhile, **Reza** *notices a piece of paper. He picks it up, reads it.*

Reza   You've written out the playlist.

Sab   Yeah?

Reza   I would have liked to have had a say.

Sab   I didn't think it'd be your thing.

Reza   Why?

Sab   I didn't think you really listened to music.

Reza *begins to laugh.*

Sab   What's so funny?

Reza   You don't think I listen to music?

Sab   No, I just thought with you being religious. You – [*didn't really listen to popular music*].

Reza   Only listened to *nasheeds* and *qawwali*?

Beat.

Sab   Most brothers don't listen to music, I just thought –

Reza   I was a stereotype of a Muslim brother that you have in your head.

Sab   I'm the last person to encourage stereotypes.

Reza   The little digs, the constant worry I'd bring *shariah* to the stage. Not every brother wants to radicalise the world.

Beat.

Sab   I'm sorry. I've been a bitch.

Reza   You really do have a good command of French.

Sab *laughs*.

Reza   I guess you have good reason to think that with Captain Hook and his gang running about.

Sab (*laughs*)   You can be quite funny.

Reza   Another surprise.

Sab   I guess I haven't had the best experience with Muslims.

Reza   Why?

Sab   They always seem to be telling you what you can't do and sending you to Hell for every little thing. Some Muslims have a superiority complex, and it doesn't matter if you're Muslim, you're not as good as them.

Reza   We're not all like that.

Sab   I know.

Reza   I wish everyone else did.

Sab   I guess I'm talking about my brother. (*Beat.*) Have you ever thought of shaving it off?

Reza   After the first attacks, having it made me feel like somehow I colluded with them. That people would think I believed what they did. I felt let down because I felt I was being asked to choose between Britishness and being a Muslim, and it's never been separate for me. (*Beat.*) I'm the kind of person – and it's a very British characteristic – I'll always side with the underdog. The underdog at the moment is a Muslim, and in an ironic way, by standing up for Muslims, I think I'm being very British. Anyway. I did come close, but I realised it's just a beard, for me it doesn't mean any of those things, for me it means something else entirely.

Sab looks at Reza.

Sab   It's weird, for me it was the other way round. My brother always used to go on and on about how I should dress more like an Asian girl. Wear a scarf on my head so people would know I was a decent girl. And I was like, I know girls who smoke, drink, sleep around, but no one thinks they have because they wear the *hijab*.

Reza *is about to speak, but* **Sab** *continues before he can say anything.*

Sab   I know not all the girls are like that. It's really weird, but if my brother had told me to wear boob tubes and a miniskirt, I probably would have worn a headscarf and everything. I nearly wore it just to give my mum some peace from constantly stopping the battle between us.

Reza   Why didn't you wear it?

Sab   I think people should be judged for what they do, and then before I could, I got offered a place at uni and I left home. I'm not really a practising Muslim like you are.

Reza   What –

Sab (*interrupting*)   Like even at uni I felt more comfortable among the non Muslims because they didn't think a skirt, or the sip of a drink, made me a bad person.

Reza   You've drank?

Sab   I know it's wrong but –

Reza   What was it like?

Sab   You want to know?

Reza   I always wondered. When did you try it?

Sab   First year of uni.

Reza   What did you have?

Sab   A lime Bacardi Breezer. And I had about six of them.

Reza   You got drunk.

Sab   Smashed. I just wanted to try it. The thing I absolutely hate about Islam is that everything is subject to interpretation. 'Consumption of alcohol is not permitted.' I'd like to know what the definition of 'alcohol' is. Like a few years ago we were told, don't wear perfume or deodorant with alcohol in it. That's just

ridiculous. Now I'm hearing from my aunt, who is actually –
I wouldn't say, 'by the book', more 'by the headline' –

Reza (*laughs*)   'By the headline', I like that –

Sab   – say, 'You can't have drink in your medicines.' I said,
'Shame – whenever I needed that little something I'd just down
the Benylin.'

Reza *laughs.*

Sab   I guess I'm not really religious like you are.

Reza   Why do you think that?

Sab   I think you have to have a bit more of a pious nature.

Reza   This is what I'm really interested by. A few minutes
ago, you said I'm not really a practising Muslim.

Sab   Yeah.

Reza   And then you said I'm not really religious.

Sab   Yeah.

Reza   And now you're saying you have to be of a pious
nature. I just want to know what makes someone a practising
Muslim? And what's this 'pious nature'? How do you know that
you don't have this pious nature?

Sab   Look, all I'm saying is –

Reza   No, I'm interested – someone who drinks, are they not
really a practising Muslim? Because I know people who, let's
say, dabble in drinking, but they also dabble a lot in praying.

Sab   Then you're not repenting. You're going through a cycle
that suits you, and your religion isn't supposed to suit you. A
lifestyle is there to suit you, but not religion. If part of religion
is sacrifice –

Reza   So you're saying you have to sacrifice things to be a
Muslim?

Beat.

Sab   I don't know what I'm saying.

Reza (*jokey*)   I think you're actually quite hard line.

Sab (*smiles*)   I don't know the answer, and I don't care so long as I don't have to debate it. That's why I avoided the Islamic Society at university, because they will argue to death. Anyway. Being tipsy was nice, an escape to a wonderful place, but, trust me, you're not missing much.

Reza   Sometimes, I wish I could escape everything.

Sab   How?

Reza   Go to the Amazon forest.

Sab   The Amazon!

Reza   It's always been a dream.

Sab   It's really beautiful.

Reza   You've been?

Sab   Yeah. I'd always wanted to go since I was a teen and I went last year, Brazil. The whole thing was amazing.

Reza   There's an exhibition on at the moment where you get to see all the early tools used in the Amazon.

Sab   Where?

Reza   At the Horniman Museum. Forest Hill.

Sab   That's brilliant. I'll have to check it out.

Reza *laughs.*

Sab   What?

Reza   I don't know many girls who'd be that enthusiastic about seeing Amazonian tools. (*Beat.*) I'm thinking of going after one of the rehearsals, do you want to come? (*Beat.*) We can see if any of the other guys want to go?

Sab   Sure, why not? It might be fun.

Blackout.

Scene Seven

Mark *and* **Sab** *sitting on the sofa.* **Sab** *is leaning against* **Mark***, her feet hanging over the sofa.* **Zain** *is sifting through a pile of CDs.*

Mark   What's taking you so long?

Zain   I can't find the CD!

Mark   I told you we should have moved on to Fire.

Zain   Yeah, and spent twenty quid on a cab home? We have to work on the charity event tomorrow, anyway. You guys would have just whinged about the music once you started coming down.

Sab   Can we just dance?

Mark   I think that CD's upstairs.

Zain   I'll go get it.

He exits.

Sab   It was a good night.

Mark   And it's not ending yet. A few more dances to –

Sab   Hits of the eighties and nineties.

Mark   I really like that new Madonna song.

He begins to sing a Madonna lyric. **Sab** *joins in.*

Sab   Hurry up, Zain!

Mark   I don't know why he arranged to meet the food suppliers on a Sunday. It's meant to be the bloody day of rest.

Sab *groans.*

Sab   I don't think I'll be able to cope.

Mark   Maybe we should get some sleep. How's it going with son of a preacher man?

Sab   His name's Reza.

Mark (*laughs*)   I'd forgotten, especially with the nickname.

Sab   He's not as bad as I thought.

Mark   So no more digs at Zain.

Sab   I can't promise no more ever.

Mark (*laughs*)   That would really be a miracle.

Pause as they listen to music.

Sab   Mark.

Mark   Yeah?

Sab   Nothing.

Mark   What?

Sab   Have you ever liked someone you never imagined liking?

Mark   Yeah, why?

Sab   Nothing. I was just wondering.

Mark *looks at* **Sab**. *He gets up.*

Mark   Do you like someone?

Sab *shakes her head.*

Mark   You like someone. (*Beat.*) Oh my fucking Lord!

Sab   What?

Mark   Admit it.

Sab   What?

Mark   You fancy him!

Sab   Who?

Mark   Son of a preacher man.

Sab   No, I don't.

Mark   I know you, Sab. Admit it.

Sab   Maybe a little.

Mark   I knew it, I knew it. Sabrina has a crush, Sabrina has a crush. ZAIN, ZAIN, Sabrina –

Sab *tries to stop* **Mark** *from calling out to* **Zain**.

Sab   Don't –

Mark   Why not? This is big – weird but big.

Sab   I don't want him to know.

Mark   You tell him everything.

Sab   This is different.

Mark   Why?

Sab   It's not supposed to happen.

Mark   You can't help who you fancy.

Sab   I don't fancy him, it's just a little crush.

Mark   Zain will be pleased.

Sab   He'll think I've lost the plot. I think I've lost the plot.

Mark   It's OK to fancy someone.

Sab   But not him.

Mark   You can't help who you fancy.

Sab   You don't understand –

Mark   Tell me what you like about him.

Sab   He's funny, really respectful – always opening doors and checking if I got home OK; making sure I'm safe not because he likes me, because he'd do that for anyone.

Mark   The problem is?

Sab   If anything was ever to happen, things would have to change. He'd expect me to give up certain things.

Mark   You always have to compromise in relationships. For the moment just enjoy liking someone.

Sab   I'm gonna get over it.

Mark   You've barely given him a chance. (*Beat.*) Zain would tell you the same thing I am. You should give this a go. Go on, tell him.

Sab   I will when there's something to tell.

Mark (*sighs*)   In the meantime don't be so quick to shut down.

Zain *comes down the stairs.*

Zain   Shut down? You're not planning to go to bed, are you?

Sab   No, I'm wide awake.

Zain   Good, because I found the CD. Let's dance.

Blackout.

Scene Eight

Models rehearsing in clothes. Music playing in the background as they rehearse their walk etc. **Sab** *is giving them instructions.* **Reza** *walks in.*

Reza   You started without me.

Sab   We literally started.

Reza   You could have waited. I was stuck in traffic.

Sab   This way everyone gets home quicker.

Reza   Are you OK?

Sab   Yeah.

Reza   You just seem a little out of sorts.

Sab   I guess I'm still tired from the week I've had.

Beat.

Reza   You didn't come to the exhibition.

Sab   Work's still hectic

She hesitates slightly.

Reza   If you want me to do more here –

Sab   It's fine. I just want these rehearsals to be efficient so we can all get home early.

Reza   Right.

They watch the models.

Sab   Great, guys, but can we get on our cues faster? We don't wanna be here all night.

Reza   I'll drive you home.

Sab   What?

Reza   I was gonna give Ali a lift. I'll drop you off on the way.

Sab   I'll be fine. (*Beat.*) I don't want to put you out.

Reza   It'll spare you the tube journey. If you really want your cortisol levels to soar, the Northern Line'll do it for you nicely.

Sab   I'll think about it.

Reza   Are you annoyed with me?

Sab   Why would I be?

Reza   I don't know.

Beat.

Sab   I'm gonna go backstage and check everything's OK. You can keep an eye here.

Sab *goes, leaving* **Reza** *confused.* **Ali** *walks in carrying a book.*

Ali   *Salaams!* I see it's all happening.

He smiles appreciatively at the models onstage.

Looks like it'll be a real good show. (*To a female model.*) Very professional.

Reza   Thanks.

Ali   Where's Sabrina?

Reza   She's gone backstage to check on the models.

Ali   Here's the leaflet, and I picked up that book. It's a bit obsessive asking me to bring it here.

Sab *walks in.*

Ali   *Salaam alakum.*

Sab   Hi.

Ali   I was just saying to Reza, this is a slick show.

Reza   We make a good team.

Silence. **Ali** *notices the awkwardness between* **Sab** *and* **Reza**.

Ali   I brought the leaflets over for you to see.

He gives one out of the box to **Sab**.

Sab   They're really good!

Ali   Did Reza tell you about our escapades handing them out this weekend?

Reza   I didn't get a chance.

Ali   Not in the past two hours?

Reza   We've been busy.

Ali (*to* **Sab**)   We drove and walked the whole of London. We handed out leaflets and posters to shops –

Reza   Universities –

Ali   Fashion colleges –

Reza   Community centres –

Ali   And in the midst of this we ended up in a museum in Forest Hill. Reza just wouldn't leave.

Reza   You enjoyed the exhibits too. The hunting equipment, the giant anaconda –

Ali   Which took all of five minutes. Three cigarette breaks later and he still wouldn't leave. I had to drag him out of there after an hour.

Sab *laughs.*

Ali   I feel sorry for the girl you end up with, you'll bore her to death.

Reza   No, I won't, I'll find a girl who likes the same things.

Ali (*shakes his head*)   Women like the finer things in life, they'll want entertainment, excitement, luxury.

Reza   That's not every girl's idea of fun. What do you think, Sab?

Beat.

Sab   I have to agree with Ali.

Ali *smiles in satisfaction and gives* **Reza** *an 'I told you so' look.* **Reza** *is confused.*

Ali   He even bought a book on the whole exhibit which he made me bring here. Reza, if you're not careful, you're gonna end up a geek.

A model shouts from out back.

Model   Guys, I need a hand.

Sab *begins to leave but before she can do so overhears:*

Reza   Ali, do you mind checking on her?

Ali   Sure.

Exit **Ali**.

Reza   Are you sure you're OK?

Sab   I'm fine.

Reza   Why didn't you turn up?

Pause.

Sab   I don't know.

Beat.

Reza *(gives her a book)*   I hope this will cheer you up a little bit and make up for the fact you missed the exhibit.

Sab   You got this for me?

Reza   I know it's not the exhibit but I thought it was unfair you missed out because of work.

Sab   You shouldn't have.

She hesitates in opening the book.

Reza   Don't you like it?

Sab   I do, I really do. Thanks a lot.

Reza   Are you sure you're OK?

Sab   Yeah, this has really cheered me up, Reza.

Beat.

Reza   Yeah.

Sab   Do you mind if I do take that offer of a lift after all?

Blackout.

Scene Nine

Mark *is watching TV. He is dressed in a cowboy outfit in the living room.* **Zain** *walks in, half dressed and holding up two shirts.*

Zain   Which one?

Mark *points to one.*

Zain   That one? I wonder what Sab's doing. She's taking ages.

Mark   I don't think she's feeling well.

Zain   What? She was fine when she walked in. (*Calls out.*) Sab, Sab!

Mark   I think we should just leave her to it.

Zain   No way. We've had this planned for ages. We're meant to be escaping everything – the nine-to-five, fashion shows. Not after I've gone to all the trouble of buying her a present.

Mark   That's really gonna make her want to come.

Zain   At least she won't have to decide what to wear.

Sab *walks in.*

Zain   Aren't you ready yet?

Mark *and* **Sab** *share a look.*

Sab   I know we had this planned, but I'm not feeling it. I may just stay home.

Zain   Come here. (*He feels her forehead for a temperature.*) You don't seem ill.

Sab   I just need the rest.

Zain   Is it the time of the month?

Sab *hits* **Zain.**

Zain   You go all weird around then. It's not PMT and not a temperature . . .

Sab   I really need to catch up with stuff for the fashion show.

Zain   No way – that wasn't the deal. Tell her, Mark.

Mark   I'm not getting involved.

Zain   You missed the last two nights out – hanging around with that brother seems to have gone to your head.

Sab   The next one, I promise.

Zain   I got you some pills.

Mark (*laughs*)   I love the way you can justify taking pills and not alcohol.

Zain   Don't encourage her. She's already jumped back on the wagon and, technically, the Qur'an says nothing about having a few Es.

Mark   I thought the word intoxicant covered it.

Sab   It doesn't matter, guys. I'm not in the mood.

Zain   I bought you a costume.

Sab   You bought me a costume?

Zain   So you have to come! I'm gonna get it.

Zain *exits.*

Sab   He bought me a costume?

Mark   Yeah. Why don't you just tell him?

Sab   That I'm going to dinner with Reza?

Mark   I don't know how you're gonna get out of this without telling Zain – especially with him getting you a costume.

Sab   What did he get me?

Mark (*laughing*)   You're gonna find out in a bit.

Sab   It's not a bunny outfit?

Mark   I think you're safe.

Zain *walks in, holding in his hands an immaculately wrapped package with a pink bow round it. He gives it to* **Sab**.

Zain   Open it.

Sab *looks at it.*

Zain   Screw the wrapping, open it.

Sab *opens the package. She pulls out a jilbab, hijab and a veil – all black.*

Sab   You're kidding.

Zain   You like it?

Sab   Funny, really funny.

Zain   Go on, try it on.

Sab   No way.

Zain   Go on.

He tries putting it on her.

Sab   Get off, get off. Mark, tell him.

Mark   I'm not getting involved.

Zain   Go on, it'll be a laugh.

Sab   No way!

Zain   Go on. Tell her, Mark.

Mark   Seriously Zain, I want no part in this.

Zain   Go on.

Sab   No.

Zain   What a waste. (*Looking at* hijab.) Are you sure?

Sab *stares at him. He picks it up.*

Zain   Be boring. I always wanted to know what it was like underneath this.

Mark   And?

Zain   I wouldn't imprison my beauty that way for the sake of any man. I'm going to get my hat.

Zain *exits.* **Mark** *hugs* **Sab.**

Mark   It was a little funny.

Beat.

Sab   A little.

Mark   Why not just make life easier on yourself and tell him?

Sab   Not now.

Mark   You have to tell him at some point.

Silence.

You shouldn't have made plans with him today.

Sab   I felt bad, especially after I let him down by not going to the exhibition.

The Pussycat Dolls' 'Buttons' begins to play loudly. **Mark** *and* **Sab** *look at each other.* **Mark** *shrugs his shoulders as if to indicate he does not know what is happening.* **Zain** *walks in with the full jilbab on, wearing red heels. He struts as if on the catwalk, does a whirl, dances provocatively in front of* **Mark** *until he moves to* **Sab,** *whom he picks up and begins to dance with.* **Zain** *separates from her and starts to remove the outfit.*

Zain   Come on, Sab, how you can resist it?

He strips off veil and throws it to her.

It's good practice for the future.

Sab   He's not like that.

Beat.

Zain   He's why you're not coming tonight.

Sab   Like I said, we're behind schedule.

Zain   Do it tomorrow. Tell him you have to cancel. He'll understand.

Sab   He's on his way.

Zain   Here?

Sab (*nods*)   To pick me up.

Zain   You're going on a date!

Silence.

You actually like this brother. (*Beat.*) Tell me this is some sort of horrible Halloween joke.

Mark   It's good for Sab –

Zain   You're so deluded, Sab.

Sab   I'm just working with him.

Zain   So, you're not falling for him?

Sab   You put us together!

Zain   Not for you to fall for him. Are you falling for him?

Silence.

Answer the question!

Sab   Don't be stupid.

Zain   Great, so you can cancel on him.

Sab   He's on his way.

Mark   Zain, leave it. It's not a crime for her to fancy someone. Anyway, she doesn't want to come. We should go, we're going to be late.

Zain   It's a party, it's fucking expected.

Mark   She's made up her mind. We should go.

Zain   Why aren't you surprised? (*Beat.*) Why aren't you surprised?

Mark   What?

Zain   Sab's just confessed to liking someone and you're not surprised, you're not – you knew. You knew about this and you didn't tell me.

Sab   It's not Mark's fault. I made him promise not to say anything.

Zain   We tell each other everything. We're meant to trust each other.

Pause.

Sab   I was going to tell you, I swear –

Zain   I can't believe you've got Muslim-girl syndrome.

Sab   Fuck off, Zain.

Zain   You're the one who's going to get your heart broken. (*Beat.*) Sure, he likes you now because you're all different and exciting, but what happens when you get married?

Sab   No one's said anything about marriage.

Zain   We both know that's where he thinks it's gonna lead, otherwise he wouldn't be going to dinner with you. Are you gonna give up everything for this guy?

Sab   He's not like that.

Zain   He's gonna let you wear skirts, club and hang round with *kafirs* like me when you go into his family home?

Sab   Things I want have changed. I want someone to come home to too.

Zain   Sure, you'll be the bad girl gone good, but in his family, you'll always be the girl who tempted him from someone better.

Mark   Zain, that's enough.

Zain   Do you want to end up in the same situation as your brother's wife? Thinking you're marrying the guy of your dreams but you end up limited to the whims of the community auntie? Staying married to someone you don't love . . . because of the neighbours next door?

Sab   I don't want to talk about this, I'm gonna get changed. (*She begins to leave.*)

Zain   Into your *shalwar kamees*?

Sab   Is this how you're going to be?

Zain (*sincerely*)   Maybe you're right, maybe he is the exception. You should have said, we could have done it properly – had a dinner party. (*Beat.*) To make him feel comfortable, we could have invited Osama, Abu Hamza, and while we're at it the whole of the Taliban. Then for dessert we could have a nice democratic vote about who they'd stone first, me or you. He's as bad as your fucking brother.

Sab   Fuck you. I'm not staying to listen to this shit. This is my damn flat too and I'll invite who I want, *mujahidin* and all. (*To* **Mark**.) Will you let me know when you leave so I know it's safe to come down?

Sab *exits.*

Silence.

Zain   Shall we go?

Silence.

You're right. No hurry. We should have a drink here instead.

He gets the drinks carrier bag, opens up the vodka, pours himself a large measure, and another which he hands to **Mark**.

Zain   We'll have a couple here – get in the mood. Music, need some music. (*Puts some house music on.*) Cigarette?

He chucks a cigarette at **Mark**, *lights his own, downs his drink, then takes a long drag of his cigarette.*

Zain   That feels good.

He begins to bop to the music. **Mark** *watches.*

Zain   We should really get into the party mood. You want a pill now?

He continues to dance, gets bored, goes back to **Mark**.

Mark   Maybe you should slow down.

Zain   We're going to a party. We're meant to be having fun.

He takes a pill. **Mark** *just stares intently at* **Zain** *and drinks.*

Mark   You were a little too much, Zain.

Zain   I was a little too much.

Mark   Why did you have to bring her brother into it? You know she hasn't spoken to him for years –

Zain   You're meant to tell me everything, that's what partners do.

Beat.

Mark   I know you're scared.

Zain   Just leave it, Mark.

Mark   I've been where you have.

Zain   What, poor little white boy Mark? Did Mummy and Daddy not speak to you for a week, two, three?

Mark   This is not about us.

Zain   The big leap out the closet isn't a three-week fucking holiday from the family for me – it's a fucking *fatwa*.

Mark   You're not the only fucking victim in the village, Zain. You need to lay off Sab, she's not the enemy.

Zain   You have no idea what you're talking about!

Mark   This is the first time in a long time she's liked someone.

Zain   He's not right for her.

Mark   You haven't given him a chance.

Zain   I know what they're like. All politically correct to the outside world, but in their houses do you think they'd accept people like you and me? If Sab wants to be a part of that world she'll have to change.

Mark   That's her choice.

Zain   She'll stop hanging about with us.

Mark   She loves you, Zain.

Zain   Me or him. They always choose their husbands.

Silence.

Mark   She's not Nadia.

Zain   She'll have no choice.

Mark   I know you're scared of losing her, but you can't –

Zain   She's one of the few people who has never batted an eyelid. One of the few people I can speak to about you.

Mark   You need to support her like she's supported you.

Silence.

You need to give him a chance for her.

Silence.

'I destroy my enemies when I make them my friends.'

Zain   I'm off Americans at the moment.

Mark   People are not black and white like the printed page of the Qur'an. Just as the words have many shades, so do people. 'We should not judge them as the ink first beholds our eye.'

Silence.

Do you remember writing that?

Beat.

Zain   Maybe you're right. Maybe I should give him a chance before I crucify him, but not tonight. We have a party to go to.

Mark   And Sab?

Zain   I'll apologise to her when she's calmer.

Mark   Make sure you don't fall out over this.

Zain   Shall we go before he turns up and the pill kicks in? Can you imagine me meeting him high?

They both laugh.

Let her know it's safe to come down.

Mark   Sab, we're leaving, babe, and Zain says he's sorry.

The men exit. As the door slams, **Sab** *walks back into the centre of the room and sits on the sofa. She picks up the hijab and looks at it. She puts the cloak and the veil in the bag, but hesitates when it comes to the hijab. She walks to the mirror with it in her hand and tentatively tries it on. She looks at herself in the mirror.*

Blackout.

Scene Ten

Reza's *house.* **Reza** *typing on his laptop.* **Ali** *walks in.*

Ali   Why you down here?

Reza   Needed the peace.

Ali   You missed Friday dinner with the lads.

Reza   I know, we needed to concentrate on the fashion –

Ali   How come I didn't get a call?

Reza   It was a little last-minute.

Ali *gets out a cigarette and lights it.*

Ali   You need to take a break. If I didn't know you better I'd think the cause here was the girl, not Palestine.

A look of guilt passes **Reza**'s *face.*

Reza I think she's got something, Ali.

Ali (*shocked*) Something?

Reza Yeah. She's intelligent, funny, passionate about justice in the world. (*Beat.*) She's really quite Islamic.

Ali What are you saying?

Reza I think she's the one. (*Beat.*) I did the *isthi'hara*!

Ali The *isthi'hara*! You only do that when you want to – It's that serious.

Reza I got a good sign.

Ali That's great, that's really great. Did you have a dream, a feeling?

Reza A dream.

Ali Who can argue with such a sign?

Reza I want the family to meet her.

Ali You're going to get married.

Reza *Inshallah.*

Ali Does she even like you?

Reza nods. **Ali** *puffs harder on his cigarette.*

Ali Have you asked her?

Reza (*shakes his head*) She knows I'm not the kind of guy to get close to her if I didn't see a future; it wouldn't be right.

Ali Right, wow. I can't believe she – I mean, I never would have thought she'd be the kind of girl you'd want to marry.

Reza It's funny what Allah has in store for you.

Ali It's great. It's good news. Have you spoken to Auntie and Uncle Nazia?

Reza I thought I'd introduce them after the fashion show.

Ali Right. This is good news. Exciting. God, you're so brave.

Reza   Brave?

Ali   I mean, I don't know how I would bring home a girl.

Reza   What?

Ali   I mean, *ammi*, all she needs is the tiniest reason to reject anyone. (*Asian accent.*) 'Marriage is not just about two people, Ali.' (*Beat.*) You're lucky your parents aren't like that. Hey, what's with the face? They'll love her.

Reza   She's not what they would have imagined.

Ali   What matters is what's in here. (*He taps his heart.*) They'll see what you see. (*Beat.*) You just have to introduce her the right way.

Reza   Yeah, you're right.

Ali   Warm them up to her before they meet. Why don't you invite her to the talk on Thursday?

Reza   At the Islamic centre?

Ali   Bhaji will be there. Introduce her as your work colleague; let her make a good impression on Bhaj independently. Bhaj will love her for being at the talk when she finds out about the charity work.

Reza   That's a great idea.

Ali   Bhaj's a good judge of character.

Reza   Yeah, she is.

Ali   I'll whisper good things in her ear.

Reza   Thanks, Ali, you're a real mate.

Ali *waves his hands as if to say, don't be silly.*

Ali   I better start organising your stag do.

Reza   It's not official yet.

Ali   I can still plan.

Reza   I'm not gonna get any work done, am I? I'll put this away and be back.

He exits with laptop, **Ali** *is left alone onstage. He lights another cigarette and smokes, deep in thought.* **Nazia** *enters with a tray of tea and biscuits.*

Ali   Bhaji.

Nazia   I bought you some *chai.* (*Begins pouring into cups.*)

Ali   You're a mind-reader.

Nazia *hands* **Ali** *his tea. He drinks it.*

Ali   You make a beautiful cup, *mashallah.* If you weren't married, your tea alone would make me propose.

Nazia *laughs.*

Nazia   Your tongue is sweeter than sugar. Have a biscuit.

Ali   Bhaji.

Nazia   Yes.

Ali   How's Reza been?

Nazia   I've barely seen him these past few weeks – he leaves early in the morning and returns when I've gone home. (*She pats her stomach.*) I get tired easily these days. He's OK?

Ali   He's fine.

Nazia   Why the question?

Ali   I think he's falling for someone.

Nazia   Reza! Who?

Ali   This girl he's working on the fashion show with.

Nazia   Sabrina?

Ali   He's spoken about her?

Nazia   He mentioned her briefly at dinner. We should book tickets for the show. What is she like? (*Beat.*) Ali, tell me!

Ali   She's nice.

Nazia   *Alhumdillah!* My little brother has been keeping secrets, that's not like him. He must like her a lot.

She laughs, but sees a worried expression cross **Ali***'s face.*

Nazia   What's wrong?

Ali   Nothing.

Nazia   Don't worry, marriage won't change things between you. It's time he – [*was settling down*].

Ali   It's not that, Bhaji.

Nazia   What is it? (*Beat.*) Ali?

Ali   I'm not sure he's making the right choice.

Nazia   *Kyu?*

Ali   I don't think I should say this.

Nazia   Ali.

Ali   Bhaji, I can't.

Nazia   Bole, I've known you since you were a baby.

Beat.

Ali   You have to promise not to tell Reza.

Nazia   You have my word.

Ali   I don't wish to taint anyone's reputation, but Sabrina . . .

Nazia   What is it?

Ali   She hit on me.

Nazia   Sabrina?

Ali   I had to push her off me.

Nazia   No.

Ali *nods in shame.*

Nazia   Have you told Reza?

Ali   He doesn't know.

Nazia   You should tell him.

Ali   He won't listen to me.

Nazia   Of course he will.

Ali   I tried to warn him off lightly in other ways. I pointed out she's a clubber, lives with two men, but – (*He shakes his head as if he can speak no further.*)

Nazia   Reza knows all this?

Ali (*nods*)   Perhaps she will change after marriage.

Nazia   I can't believe Reza would like someone like that. I'll speak to him.

Ali   No, Bhaji, then he will know I have interfered. Maybe you should meet her yourself before Reza introduces her to the family.

Nazia   But how?

Ali   She's coming to the talk this Thursday. You can see her then.

Nazia   Thanks, Ali, thanks a lot.

Blackout.

Scene Eleven

An Islamic talk. **Sab** *is facing the audience. She joins in a round of applause, and as she does so looks around. She is clearly nervous.* **Zain** *approaches from* **Sab**'s *blind spot. He is wearing sunglasses. He puts his hand on* **Sab** *shoulder, and she jumps.*

Sab   What are you doing here?

Zain   You know me, there's no other way I'd like to spend an evening than to be at an Islamic talk.

Beat. They share an awkward silence.

Mark told me what was happening.

Sab   So?

Zain   I thought you might need a friend. (*Beat.*) I know things haven't been great between us, but I wouldn't torture myself like this for just anyone.

Sab   Thanks.

Zain   Don't be silly. I could hardly pass up the opportunity of seeing you meet the holy crew. This is way too good to miss.

They both laugh.

Sab   I'm sorry I never said anything about Reza. No more secrets.

Zain   No more secrets? It's gonna be a dull life.

Sab   Can you take off those sunglasses?

Zain   Why?

Sab   I can't see what your eyes are doing.

Zain   So?

Sab   I can't see what you're actually thinking.

Zain   Don't be stupid.

Sab *moves and grabs* **Zain**'s *sunglasses off him.*

Zain   I think you should behave. Three o'clock, your boyfriend and entourage are approaching. Smile.

Reza   *Salaam alakum.*

Zain   *Walakum salaam.* (*Shakes hands.*)

Ali   *Salaam alakum.*

Zain   *Walakum salaam.* (*Shakes hands, goes to shake hands with* **Nazia**, *but she doesn't.*) *Salaam*, sorry I wasn't thinking. (*He looks at* **Sab**.)

Nazia   *Walakum salaam*, no problem.

Reza   Bhaj, this is Sab who I have been working with, and Zain, the organiser of the festival.

Nazia   *Alhumdillah*, Reza's told me what a good job you're doing for a worthy cause. Awful what is happening in Palestine.

Zain   It's horrible. I hope we will be able to help in some small way.

Nazia   I'm looking forward to the whole event; we've already bought our tickets. It'll be nice to see what my little brother has done.

Reza   Most the work has been down to Sab.

Nazia   Yes, so Ali has told me.

Reza *gives a look of appreciation to* **Ali**.

Nazia   I do hope Reza has been doing his fair share.

Sab (*nods*)   We make a good team.

Reza *and* **Sab** *smile at each other*.

Nazia   Good to know Reza is committed to his charity work as usual.

Ali   Did you enjoy the talk?

Sab   It was interesting.

Zain (*nods*)   Interesting.

Nazia   I was surprised by some of the views.

Reza   It's healthy to have debate, Bhaj.

Nazia   The second speaker was –

Ali   Asking women to take off the headscarf.

Nazia   It's a bit much.

Zain   I thought he had some interesting points. Finally, a *fatwa* not condemning someone to death. It'll be good for our image.

A dull silence. **Sab** *glares at* **Zain**.

Zain   I was joking. (*An awkward laugh.*) If the *hijab* is making women targets for violence, then maybe they should consider removing it – for their safety.

Reza   Logically his argument makes sense, but it would be nice if there was another way.

Ali   It is the sisters who are the victims here; it's the public who needs educating.

Zain   If it lets them walk around freely without the fear of a backlash, then they should.

Nazia   You're right. I could never imagine taking off my *hijab*, whatever the circumstances. It's integral to a woman's identity as a Muslim.

Zain   I thought belief in Allah and the Prophet were integral.

Ali   There are codes of conduct which we must follow.

Zain   Most of these codes of conduct are open to interpretation.

Reza   That's why talks like these are so great – they allow people to interpret things in so many ways.

Ali   Wearing the *hijab* is a virtuous act.

Zain   Not wearing a *hijab* doesn't make you any less of a Muslim than one who does.

Reza   No one says it does.

Zain   Everyone knows wearing a *hijab* makes a woman virtuous and others less so.

Ali   It's a duty.

Zain   I thought it was optional.

Reza   I guess you guys subscribe to different schools of thought.

Nazia   What do you think, Sabrina?

Sab   I have a lot of respect for women who wear it, but I think people can be just as religious without it.

Nazia   You share a view similar to your friend. How did the two of you meet?

Zain *and* **Sab** *look at each other. They take a little too long to answer.*

Ali   You live together, don't you?

Zain   We met at university.

Ali   I must be mistaken, I thought –

Sab   We're flatmates.

Zain   Rent is so expensive nowadays, you have no choice but to share.

Nazia   Your families don't mind?

Sab   Zain's like family.

Reza   Bhaji, there's three of them living together.

Nazia   So you live with one of your relatives?

Zain   We live with another guy.

Nazia   It's so strange, I never thought for a second to move out of my family home before I was married.

Reza   Sabrina's from Manchester, Bhaji. She can't commute to work. Sabrina's job has really helped us make this show. She's been able to call in a few favours.

Nazia   You've been very lucky. I was surprised when Reza told me what you did.

Sab   Why?

Nazia   It's something that white girls usually do.

Zain *tries to hold back an 'I told you so' look at* **Sab**, *who recognises the hidden dig.* **Ali** *smiles.* **Reza** *is shocked at his sister.*

Reza   Bhaji!

Zain   I guess we could say that about all jobs once upon a time.

Nazia   Of course, you're right. Someone has to make the first step into new territories, but it can be hard for those around you. What did your parents say about your job?

Sab *looks at* **Zain**, *then at* **Reza** *and back to* **Nazia**.

Sab   They were resistant to it at first.

Reza   But they're fine now. They're coming down for the fashion show, aren't they?

Nazia *looks at* **Sab** *questioningly.*

Sab   Yes, yes, they are.

Nazia (*nods*)   The hours must be long.

Reza   That's a hazard of working in the City.

Nazia   I keep saying to Reza, he has to find a job where the hours are shorter. When he gets married he can't leave his wife for hours waiting for him to return.

Sab   That wouldn't be ideal.

Zain   He might not have to; she might be working long hours as well.

Nazia   Mum and Dad are looking for a good girl for him to settle down with. I am sure they'll do a good job. They did with introducing the rest of us to our partners. Just the baby left.

Reza   Bhaji.

Sab   If you'll excuseme, I'm going to use the Ladies.

A few seconds after **Sab** *leaves:*

Zain   Excuse me.

He follows **Sab**, *who's slightly ahead of him.*

Zain   Sab, Sab.

Sab *turns around.*

Zain   Are you OK?

Sab *nods.*

Zain   Talk about a pit bull in a headscarf.

Silence.

Sab   It was just meant to be a friendly meeting.

Zain   If that's how she's to his friends, you're better off out of it. (*Sees* **Sab***'s face.*) He wasn't the one spouting the crap, I suppose.

Sab   He wasn't, was he?

Zain   He wasn't exactly telling her to shut up either.

Sab   I'm gonna use the Ladies.

Zain   Do you want to go home?

Sab   I'm gonna get some fresh air.

Zain   Do you want me to come with you?

Sab (*shakes her head*)   I just need a few minutes.

Spotlight moves back to **Reza**, **Nazia** *and* **Ali**.

Reza   Why did you have to say that thing about getting married?

Nazia   Why shouldn't I have said it?

Reza   It's just a little embarrassing. Makes us seem a bit backward.

Nazia   Chup. They're Muslim, they understand, and if they think that, don't worry, in a few months, you will barely see them, the conversation will be forgotten.

Reza   Maybe.

Nazia   Maybe?

Reza   I may do some charity work with them.

Nazia   That's good. Who knows, you might meet a girl to marry through it.

Reza   I already have.

Nazia   What?

Reza   I like Sabrina.

Nazia *laughs.*

Reza   Why are you laughing?

Nazia   Because you're joking.

Reza   I'm thinking of introducing her to Mum and Dad.

Pause.

Nazia　I see. How would you explain her lifestyle before she met you?

Ali　Bhaji.

Nazia　Ali, give Reza and me a minute.

Ali　Of course.

He exits.

Nazia　How would you explain her lifestyle before she met you?

Reza　They don't have to know.

Nazia　You'd lie to them?

Reza　No.

Nazia　What else wouldn't you tell them?

Reza　I didn't mean – [*that the way it sounded*].

Nazia　Reza.

Nazia　Realistically, if she's to be your wife, she will have to make big changes, Reza. Will she?

Silence.

It is a part of life to be attracted to people, but you must think about what's best for you, your *deen*, your family.

Reza　I know, Bhaj, but once you get to know her you'll realise she's similar to us.

Nazia　Reza, you're such a decent guy. I could see why any girl would want you, but you can't believe everything everyone tells you. She lives alone with that boy.

Reza　They're just flatmates.

Nazia　The way he ran after her. It felt like they were . . .

Silence.

At the end of the day we will trust your judgement. If you think she will fit in with the family, then fine. But you know there

are other options. Mum and Dad introduced me to Imran.
I couldn't be happier.

Silence.

We have to be the example, Rez.

Reza   I value your opinion, Bhaj.

Silence.

Nazia   I hope I haven't said anything wrong.

Reza *shakes his head.*

Nazia   If it is destined to be it will be. Do what you feel is right.

Fade out. Spotlight onto **Sab**, *who is waiting outside.* **Ali** *comes out. He looks at* **Sab**. *She ignores him. He lights a cigarette.*

Ali   Do you mind?

Sab   Go ahead.

Ali *begins smoking,* **Sab** *ignores him, starts to walk away. He offers her a cigarette.*

Ali   Would you like one?

Sab   No.

Ali   How's your evening been?

Sab (*going to leave*)   Fine.

Ali   I was surprised to see you here.

Sab   Were you?

Ali   A pleasant surprise.

Silence.

The only thing with work and the time of these things is you
never really get a chance to eat, do you?

Sab   Not really.

Ali   You must be hungry.

Sab   I'll eat when I get home. (*Begins to leave.*)

Ali   Why wait?

Sab   What?

Ali   We can go get something to eat.

Sab   No thanks.

Ali   You seem a little upset.

Sab   I'm fine.

Ali   Join me for dinner.

Sab   I'm not hungry.

Ali   We could get to know each other. You'll see I'm really a nice guy, and then –

Sab   Then what?

Ali   What life brings.

Sab   What life brings.

Ali   We're both adults. (*He looks at her and stubs out his cigarette.*) Some harmless enjoyment never hurt anyone.

Sab   I'm not interested in being your whore.

Ali   But you are in being Reza's.

Sab   Fuck you!

Ali   What's the difference between us? We're the same, him and me. In fact, I'm more likely to give you what you want. Reza is too straight and yellow for that. Why not me? I would treat you well.

Sab   You want me to be your wife?

Ali   We both know that's unrealistic.

Sab   Unrealistic.

Ali   Our lifestyles wouldn't be compatible, but there are other options.

Sab *begins to walk away.* **Ali** *stops her by blocking her path.*

Ali   I'd treat you well – the best restaurants, the most expensive shops. There's nothing stopping us from enjoying ourselves.

Sab   God.

Ali   He forgives.

Sab *(stares at him)*   You make me sick. You'll have to get your thrills elsewhere. I'm not for sale.

She turns and walks away. **Ali** *is disappointed but recovers quickly.*

Ali   You're a dime a dozen. I'll pick you up tomorrow on the street corner.

She ignores him and carries on walking out.

Blackout.

Scene Twelve

Reza *in his office on the phone. He has a laptop in front of him.*

Reza *(on phone)*   I've scheduled us to audit the McMinn Enterprises on the thirteenth of this month. We will hold a meeting on – *(Knock at door.)* Come in. *(Back to phone and computer screen.)* The twentieth, great. See you then.

He looks up. **Sab** *stands in front of him. He is visibly shocked.*

Reza   Sab. *(Beat.)* What are you doing here?

Sab   I needed to see you.

Reza   You look . . . well.

Silence.

Sab   You haven't responded to my phone calls or emails.

Reza   It's been manic at work.

Sab   You missed the rehearsal yesterday.

Reza   Sorry, I picked up the message late.

Sab   There's one tonight.

Reza   I'm not sure I'll be able to make it. I'm working on this really intense project and I'm not sure if −

Sab   Why didn't you ring me when you found out?

Reza   I thought I might be able to reschedule. (*Beat.*) I just don't think I can be as involved as I was.

Sab   Right.

Reza   I'm happy to hand out leaflets, spread the word.

Sab *nods.*

Reza   I'll do what I can.

Beat.

Sab   You sure have the corporate persona down to a T.

Reza   What?

Sab   Couldn't you have thought of something more original?

Silence.

Why don't you just say it?

Reza   What?

Sab   Just say it.

Reza   What, Sab?

Sab   We both know this isn't about the fashion show. (*Pause.*) You've gone cold on me since . . . (*Begins to get emotional, then controls herself.*) I just want to hear the words.

Reza   What do you want me to say?

Sab   That you're scared.

Reza   Scared?

Sab   Too weak to pursue someone who hasn't had the seal of approval.

Reza   It's not that.

Sab   It's certainly not some bullshit project.

Silence.

Reza   I realised I gave you the wrong impression.

Sab   Wrong impression?

Reza   That my feelings for you were more than just friends. I thought it was best to distance – [*myself*].

Sab   Be a coward and avoid my calls.

Reza   No, yes. I just wanted some time to think.

Sab   And?

Reza   I think we inhabit different worlds.

Sab   What does that mean?

Reza   I don't think we're suited.

Sab   You didn't think that a few weeks ago.

Silence.

Reza   We're just looking for different things.

Sab   What are you looking for?

Reza   Someone, someone.

He looks at **Sab** *as if to say it is she he is looking for.* **Sab** *does not register the look.*

Sab   Someone who's a poster girl for Islam?

Reza   No.

Sab   This is bullshit.

Reza   Sab, I'm sorry.

Silence.

Sab (*struggling with the words*)   If I wore the *hijab*?

Reza   What?

Sab Would that make it easier?

Reza Sab.

Sab Would it make it easier? (*Beat.*) Would it?

Reza Yes.

Sab If that's what it takes then – [*I'll do it*].

Reza Don't do this.

Sab If I did it, then why not?

Reza Sab.

Sab Why not?

Reza You wouldn't be happy.

Sab I'd do it for you.

Reza It's not that simple. I'm sorry, Sabrina.

Sab What else is there?

Reza You and Zain.

Sab What about us?

Reza How am I gonna explain that?

Sab We're flatmates.

Reza I should have realised how close you were. When my sister said –

Sab But he's, he's – he's just a good friend, trust me.

Reza I always thought my wife would be –

Silence.

Sab Would be what?

Reza Sab, I have to worry about my family's reputation. People would believe –

Sab Fuck them, this is about you and me.

Silence.

We work, Reza, we work.

Reza   I can't do it, Sab.

Sab *reaches for him but* **Reza** *walks away.*

Sab   So that's it? You're just gonna –

Reza   You'll find someone else, someone better.

Sab   You're right, it's best I know now, you're just like the rest of them. Too scared to challenge the crowd. Too scared to stand up for more than one version of a Muslim. Too scared to ask me if I've fucked Zain.

Reza (*winces*)   Sab!

Sab   Would it matter if I had? I wouldn't have cared if you had. I wouldn't have judged you. That would have been the past. I honestly thought you were – (*Laughs.*) More fool me. I don't need this bullshit. You know what's really funny? Ali turned out to be more honest than you. Goodbye, Reza.

She begins to leave.

Reza   Sab.

She doesn't look back. **Reza** *looks at the door, slowly gets up, closes the door. Leans against it and closes his eyes.*

Blackout.

Scene Thirteen

Zain *and* **Mark** *in the flat.*

Mark   *EastEnders* is on in ten minutes.

Zain   So?

Mark   They're going to get together.

Zain   Why does he fancy her? She looks like a smashed pumpkin.

Mark   They're an odd couple.

Zain   Like Clive and Thomas.

Mark   They're sweet.

Zain   That's because you never have a bad word to say about anyone.

Mark   They're getting married.

Zain   It seems everyone's got the bug. Imagine marrying Clive. (*He shudders.*) I'd rather do Mr Burns from *The Simpsons*.

Mark (*laughs*)   It's sweet, they're making a commitment.

Zain   Thomas is a gold-digger.

Mark   You are so cynical.

Zain   He's marrying a corpse. What twenty-two-year-old gay guy goes out with a forty-year-old?

Mark (*laughs*)   Sab was worried about being over the hill. I can't believe we're as bad.

Zain   It's a dog-eat-dog world.

Mark   Zain, do you ever see us –

Beat.

Zain   Us?

Mark   You know –

He makes head gestures. **Zain** *looks as him, puzzled.*

Mark   – getting married?

Zain *laughs.* **Mark** *is visibly upset by the response.*

Zain   You're being serious.

Mark *nods. Silence.*

Zain   You and me?

Mark   Just forget it, it was stupid.

Zain   God, no, it's just that I never imagined – I mean, I never thought I'd ever get married.

Mark *looks upset.*

Zain   You know how I feel about you. It's just with everything I never thought –

Mark   I can't believe you're giving Sab such a hard time.

Zain   What?

Mark   At least Sab has the courage of her convictions.

Zain   What?

Mark   She knew you wouldn't like it; his family might not like her but she still put herself out there, tried to change the status quo. I'm going to get some cigarettes.

Zain *looks shocked as if he can't quite work out what has happened. He recovers a few seconds after* **Mark** *has left the flat.*

Zain   Mark, Mark! (*He pulls out his phone and makes a call. He cuts off his phone.*) Great fucking job, Zain.

He walks towards the door and opens it. **Sab** *walks in.* **Zain** *stays at the door.*

Zain   Bloody hell, Sab, you scared the life out of me.

Sab   Why you standing in the doorway?

Zain   Did you see Mark?

Sab   On the way in. He said he was heading to the shop.

Zain   Did he look OK?

Sab   Yeah.

Zain   He said he'd be back?

Sab   *EastEnders*'s on in a minute.

Zain   Did he say he was coming back for it?

Sab   I didn't ask.

Zain *stays at the door.*

Sab   What's going on?

Zain   I've been a fuckwit.

Sab   What happened?

Zain   We had an argument.

Sab   About?

Zain   He asked me to marry him.

Sab   Seriously?!

Zain *nods.*

Sab   That's brilliant.

Zain (*sighs*)   I laughed, Sab.

Sab   You didn't?!

Zain *nods.*

Sab   Poor Mark.

She comforts **Zain**.

Zain   I always thought I'd marry a woman.

Sab   What?

Zain   I always thought this was a phase. When I realised it wasn't, I decided I'd never get married. Imagine doing that to some poor cow from back home. When he said it, Sab, I don't know, it was funny and scary, me marrying Mark. (*Beat.*) That'd mean I'd be completely out of the loop, wouldn't I?

Sab   No, you'd still have me.

Zain   Something so official – it feels like choosing sides.

Sab   It's never that simple.

Zain   All I saw was the *dohl* playing, a grand stage and both of us fighting over the wedding dress. Imagine that?

Sab (*laughs*)   That'd be one hell of an Asian wedding! (*She is trying to hold back the tears.*)

Zain   Sab?

Sab   You better make it up with him. He's a great guy, and he's probably one of the few guys who mean it. I want to be bridesmaid.

Zain   Hey, we could get married on the same day – you marrying the brother and me Mark. Now that would be the talk of the century.

Sab *can no longer stop the tears.*

Zain   Why the tears? Mark and I will be fine.

Sab   You were right.

Zain   About me being a fuckwit? Hey, I know that may come as a shock, but I'm just mortal too.

Sab *laughs through her tears.*

Sab   Reza.

Zain *looks at* **Sab**.

Sab   He's not doing the show.

Zain   Why?

Sab   He thinks we're not suited.

Zain   To get married?

Sab   His family.

Zain   What a typical spineless Asian wanker. You're worth ten of them.

Sab   Maybe.

Zain   Why are you so insecure?

Sab   Everybody needs a hobby.

Zain (*laughs*)   One of you is worth a million of the God gang.

*He hugs **Sab** and rocks her back and forth. **Mark** walks back in, a six-pack of Stella in his hands.*

Zain   Can I have one?

Mark   Is everything OK?

Zain   Son of a preacher man has just pulled out of the show and –

Sab   – dumped me.

Zain   Technically you can only be dumped if you've kissed a person.

*He squeezes **Sab** comfortingly.*

Mark   What did he say?

Sab   We inhabited different worlds.

Mark   Stupid fucker.

Sab   The most ridiculous thing was he thought that Zain and I were – (*Making a gesture as if to say 'sleeping together'.*) You know.

Zain / Mark   What!

Zain   Why?

Sab   We live together.

Mark   You should have told him Zain was gay. (*Beat.*) I wasn't thinking.

Pause.

Zain (*looks at **Mark***)   You could have told him, Sab.

Sab   I shouldn't have had to.

Zain   It always the same story. (*Pause.*) Do you want me to send them a copy of one of Sarah Maple's paintings? That'll stir them right up!

Sab (*laughs*)   Don't be stupid. (*Pause.*) God, I need someone to present the fashion show with me. I'm gonna have to call people –

Zain (*in mock horror*)   Call people, call people, when the perfect man is right here? I was born for the role. I will have more charisma in my little finger than in the whole of preacher boy's being.

Sab (*laughs*)   Thanks, Zee. I just wish you could sort out everything else so easily.

Zain   You know you can always marry me – I'm allowed four partners –

He reaches out for **Mark**, *puts one arm round him, the other round* **Sab**.

Zain   – but being married to Mark and you I think I could settle with just the two.

He kisses **Sab** *on the head.*

Blackout.

Scene Fourteen

Reza *in his office, typing.* **Ali** *sitting on a chair.*

Reza   Give me five minutes and we can go.

Ali   You just need to get back to the old routine.

Reza   Yeah.

Ali   Get some fresh air, play football with the lads.

Reza   I'm fine.

A knock at the door.

That was quick.

They laugh.

(*Still packing away.*) Come in.

Zain *walks in.* **Reza** *is surprised.*

Ali   *Salaam alakum.*

Zain *refuses to shakes his hand and does not respond.* **Reza** *turns round.*

Reza   *Salaam alakum.*

Silence.

I'm surprised to see you here.

Zain   I wanted to speak to you.

Ali   We're on our way to *jummah*.

Zain   It won't take long.

Reza   It's fine.

Silence. It drags on a little too long for comfort.

Do you want to speak in private?

Zain   No, he can stay.

Reza   If you're here to speak about the fashion show –

Zain   I'm here about Sab.

Silence.

Reza   Is she OK?

Zain   You shouldn't have led her to believe something could happen between the two of you.

Reza   I made a mistake.

Zain   You chickened out.

Reza   I'll speak to Sab again, make sure she understands.

Zain   She understands. She got the message loud and clear. She'll get through it.

Ali   She does have you to comfort her.

Reza   I'm sorry if I hurt her.

Ali   Don't apologise, you made the right choice.

Zain   As much as I hate to say it, I agree with him.

Ali   Then why are you here?

Zain I came here to set the record straight.

Reza About what?

Zain My relationship with Sab. Sab and I are just friends.

Ali You expect us to believe that? The maths doesn't add up.

Zain Well, we are.

Ali I believe the correct term is friends with advantages.

Zain I'm with Mark.

Ali You brought him here as a witness? Of course he's going to agree –

Zain He's not here. I'm with Mark, not Sabrina.

Silence and confused looks.

Ali You mean you and Mark are – (*Puts his middle finger over his index finger.*)

Zain Yes.

*A look of disgust passes over **Ali**'s and **Reza**'s faces, but just as quickly another emotion replaces it.*

Ali B-b-but, b-b-but, but you're Muslim – (*To **Reza**.*) This is worse than we thought.

Beat.

Reza (*to **Zain***) So, she's never had a re— [*lationship with you*]?

Zain No.

Reza And you're definitely – ?

Zain Yes.

Reza Oh God.

Ali You're so much better without her. Look at who she would have brought into your home. You were spared.

Zain (*to **Ali***) I can't believe you ever thought Sabrina would go out with you.

Reza   What?

Zain   You mean he didn't tell you he asked her out?

Reza   Ali?

Ali   You don't believe him, do you?

Reza   Did you?

Ali   You know me.

Pause.

Reza   You're lying.

Ali   Reza, this is me.

Reza   You're lying.

Ali   I only did it so you could keep your *izaat*. She was unsuitable.

Zain   That's why she had to turn you down twice.

Reza   Twice?

Ali   You're going to take this *shai'tan*'s word over mine? Do you think he's going to worry about lying when he's committing the worst sin of them all?

Zain   I haven't got anything else to lie about.

Beat as **Reza** *realises the truth of* **Zain**'s *words.*

Reza   You're meant to be my friend.

Ali   Reza, I swear on Allah –

Reza   Don't! Don't!

Ali   I did it for you.

Reza   For me? (*Beat.*) I think you should leave for *jummah*.

Ali   Are you coming?

Reza   On your own, Ali.

Ali   She would have embarrassed you.

Reza   Get out.

Ali   I did you a favour, you don't know where to box people. She would have made your father's standing in the community –

Reza   Get out!

Ali   You want to be left alone with him?

Reza   GO!

Ali *hesitates, but leaves.* **Zain** *and* **Reza** *are left alone. Pause as* **Reza** *recovers himself.*

Reza   I'm sorry.

Zain   It's not me you have to say sorry to.

Reza   I owe you both an apology. I'll call her.

Zain   Don't.

Reza   What?

Zain   I didn't come here for that. I came here so you'd know the truth. God does not judge according to your bodies and appearance, but He scans your hearts and looks into your deeds.

Reza   The Prophet was a wise man.

Zain   He was. Maybe if we listened to him we wouldn't be so quick to try and judge each other. I thought you of all people would know that.

Silence.

Reza   I've been an idiot.

Zain   Sab deserves someone better.

Silence.

Reza   Will you tell her I'm sorry?

Zain *nods.*

Zain   I think it's time I left.

Reza   I'll walk you out.

Zain   It's fine, but before I leave I hope you understand everything I said about myself was meant for these four walls.

Reza   No one will know anything from me, but as for Ali, I can't guarantee he'll do the same.

Zain   That's all I can ask for.

Reza (*nods*)   Thank you.

Zain (*surprised*)   For what?

Reza   For telling me the truth. It couldn't have been easy.

Zain   I'm sorry things couldn't have worked out differently for you.

Reza *and* **Zain** *shake hands.* **Zain** *walks to the door, but hesitates and turns back.*

Zain   I have to also say –

Reza   Yes?

Zain   I think it would be for the best if you and your family didn't turn up for the event.

Reza   But –

Zain   I think she's been hurt enough. (*Silence.*) I'll refund any tickets.

Reza   There's no need, it's the least I can do.

Zain (*nods*)   So, we're agreed?

Reza *looks at* **Zain.** *Unable to trust his voice, he nods his agreement.*

Blackout.

Scene Fifteen

The fashion show. **Sab** *in a long, black, strapless dress,* **Zain** *in a suit.*

Zain (*flicks his collars*)   Smoking!

Sab   Have you been checking on the models or looking in the mirror?

Zain *coughs, does a twirl, coughs again.*

Zain   All's fine and dandy, Captain. (*Salutes.*)

Sab   Great.

Pause.

Zain   You OK?

Sab *nods.*

Zain   Don't be nervous (*putting his arm around her*), cos no one's going to be looking at you even if you do fuck up because all eyes will be on me.

Sab *hits him.*

Zain   I do look good. (*Holds his arms out.*) I look good, go on, say it.

Sab (*laughs*)   You look good.

Zain   The lady had impeccable taste. You going to be OK?

Sab   I am the professional organiser here.

Zain   Sab.

Sab   I'll be fine.

Mark *walks in.*

Mark   Five minutes, guys. You OK, doll?

Sab   I wish you guys would stop asking me that – makes me feel like I'm terminally ill or something.

Zain   Shall we get this show on the road then?

*He takes **Sab** by the arm and twirls her round.*

Zain (*to **Mark***)   See you soon.

Mark   I'll be here, getting the models prepped.

Zain   Remember to crack open the champagne on our return.

Mark   Dom Perignon all the way.

Zain *and* **Sab** *exit.* **Mark** *is left onstage.*

Mark   Ladies and gents, let's go.

A girl dressed in a sari gets ready to move onto the stage. A song plays. After a while, we see **Reza** *walk backstage.* **Mark** *spots him and stops him before he can walk on with the models.*

Mark   You're a little late, aren't you?

Reza   I've come to speak to Sabrina.

Mark   She's busy running an event you should have been helping her with.

Reza   I'll wait here for her.

Mark   I think you should leave.

Reza   I need to speak to her.

Mark   Not here.

Reza   It's important.

Sab *and* **Zain** *return in conversation. They spot* **Reza**. **Sab** *is visibly shaken,* **Zain** *annoyed.* **Reza** *and* **Sab** *look at each other.*

Zain   I think you should leave.

Reza   Sabrina –

Sab   We need to get on with the show. I'm gonna wait by the side of the stage for our cue.

Reza *blocks her exit.*

Reza   Sabrina, I'm really sorry for thinking those things, I should have –

Sab   It's in the past.

Reza   I just want you to know if I could rewind time . . . I can't believe I ever thought . . .

Sab   You're forgiven, OK. There's no need to feel guilty.

Reza   Sabrina, I need to explain. I just want to talk to you and make you see –

Sab   What's left to say? You shouldn't have come here.

Reza   I've been an idiot. I made a huge mistake.

Sab   I can't do this. (*She begins to walk offstage.*)

Reza   I want you to meet my family. My parents want to meet you.

Mark *and* **Zain** *look at* **Reza** *with respect.*

Sab   I'm not gonna be the girl who pushed you off your pedestal.

Reza   You don't understand. I've spoken –

Sab   You'll find someone better.

Reza   I don't think I will.

Sab   It's all over with. You were right, we're looking for different things.

Reza   Just give me a minute.

Sab   I said it's over! Just go. (*Beat.*) Please.

Reza *looks at* **Sab** *and exits. Beat as* **Sab** *struggles with her emotions.* **Mark** *and* **Zain** *look at each other.* **Mark** *walks up to* **Sab** *and puts his arm round her.*

Mark   I thought that was pretty romantic.

Sab   Not now, Mark.

Mark   Why don't you go after him and give him a chance to say his piece? What he did was really sweet.

Sab   Mark.

Mark   It must have been really hard for him.

Sab   I'm going to take my position offstage. You coming, Zain?

Zain   Sab. He didn't have to come here to apologise, especially after we told him not to. That's sweet even for a brother.

Mark *smiles at* **Zain.**

Sab   Zain?

Zain   Admittedly, it was all a little Bollywood, but I think you should go talk to him.

Sab   We're in the middle of the show.

Zain   I have enough personality to command the stage for both of us. You were holding me back anyway.

Sab   Why are you defending him?

Zain   Sometimes we make mistakes, Sab. Sometimes, when we should say yes we get scared and fuck things up. Sometimes we don't do the thing we know we should do. He's trying to do the right thing. It's better late than never.

Sab   I don't want to go through it all again.

Zain   You don't have to. Just hear him out.

Silence. He puts his arm round **Sab**.

Zain   Whatever happens, we'll be right here when you come back.

Sab *begins to leave but hesitates.*

Zain   Go on, go!

Sab   Thanks, Zee.

Sab *walks off the stage.*

Blackout.